FRESH FROM
LOUISIANA

FRESH FROM
LOUISIANA

THE SOUL OF CAJUN
AND CREOLE HOME COOKING

RECIPES, STORIES, AND PHOTOGRAPHS BY
GEORGE GRAHAM

Author of *Acadiana Table*

HARVARD
COMMON
PRESS

DEDICATION

TO MY WIFE ROXANNE:
YOUR HERITAGE OF CAJUN COOKING
THROUGH THE STORIES YOU TELL OF GROWING UP
IN A GODLY HOME HAS INSPIRED ME
TO PRESERVE THEM
FOR FUTURE GENERATIONS.

Inspiring | Educating | Creating | Entertaining

Brimming with creative inspiration, how-to projects, and useful information to enrich your everyday life, Quarto Knows is a favorite destination for those pursuing their interests and passions. Visit our site and dig deeper with our books into your area of interest: Quarto Creates, Quarto Cooks, Quarto Homes, Quarto Lives, Quarto Drives, Quarto Explores, Quarto Gifts, or Quarto Kids.

First Published in 2020 by The Harvard Common Press, an imprint of The Quarto Group, 100 Cummings Center, Suite 265-D, Beverly, MA 01915, USA.
T (978) 282-9590 F (978) 283-2742 QuartoKnows.com

The Harvard Common Press titles are also available at discount for retail, wholesale, promotional, and bulk purchase. For details, contact the Special Sales Manager by email at specialsales@quarto.com or by mail at The Quarto Group, Attn: Special Sales Manager, 100 Cummings Center, Suite 265-D, Beverly, MA 01915, USA.

24 23 22 21 20   1 2 3 4 5

ISBN: 978-1-59233-976-1

Digital edition published in 2020
eISBN: 978-1-63159-922-4

Library of Congress Control Number: 2020942794

Design and Page Layout: Amy Sly
Photography: George Graham except as follows: Roxanne Graham, page 234

Printed in China

INTRODUCTION
A ROAD MAP OF LOUISIANA COOKING

Thanks for joining me on my journey of discovering what makes Louisiana cooking so unique. In the pages of *Fresh from Louisiana*, I've delivered a road map of the culinary delights that await you and the fresh ingredients that will astound you. Eating in the South is tied to the seasons, and Louisiana is no exception. The recipes I've chosen for this book are divided that way to ensure the freshest ingredients are available during the respective growing season. Farm fresh is the cultural mandate of Louisiana cooking and the essence of what sets it apart. As a child, I learned to anticipate the market seasons: Ponchatoula strawberries in the spring, Creole tomatoes in the summer, Evangeline sweet potatoes in the fall, and a pot full of farm-fresh collards in the winter. And the Louisiana soil I grew up on delivered.

WELCOME TO A SECOND HELPING OF LOUISIANA COOKING

I plan to show you the places I know and introduce you to the people I've met that make Louisiana's culinary culture so colorful. If you read my first book, *Acadiana Table*, then rest assured that this next one will take a deeper dive as I crisscross the state in pursuit of the stories behind the recipes.

I've had a lifelong love affair with the food culture of Louisiana. I love the recipes living inside this cookbook for the history that calls me back to the table and for the ties that bind me to memories of food and family. I love the way a spicy crawfish pie weaves its lyrical melody and sings to me with a Doug Kershaw accent, how a pork and pork-and-apple-stuffed duck is only a vessel for the sweet, duck fat–roasted onions that accompany it, and how the perfumed scent of fresh basil wafts from a crispy-crusted Creole tomato tart as it comes out of a hot oven.

MY CULINARY EDUCATION

Louisiana food is soulful; it is part of who I am, where I come from, what I'm made of.

I grew up in Bogalusa, where Louisiana straddles Mississippi, and only the Pearl River separates the two. It was just one hour north of New Orleans but a world away from the fun and funk of its spicy gumbo pot of culinary wonders. Bogalusa was pimento cheese between two slices of Holsum bread; New Orleans was a sloppy, ten-napkin roast beef nestled in a crusty Leidenheimer loaf.

The only thing that saved this country boy from a bland upbringing was the fact that my father was a restaurant man. He was a 24-hour-a-day, 364-day-a-year restaurant man who dished up the tastiest meat-and-three blue plates between Jackson and the Big Easy. And it was hard work feeding travelers, shoppers, and the four thousand paper mill workers at the plant that backed up to the Acme Café on Columbia Road. My father had grease running through his veins and a tireless work ethic that shaped my culinary world and filled me with a curious appetite to know more.

Watching the cooks in my father's restaurant, I learned what any aspiring chef should know. To some, a twelve year old working in a restaurant kitchen would seem a forthright reason to call child protection services. To me, it was a privilege, a blessing. I learned more about cooking standing atop a wooden orange crate and peering over an eight-burner Garland range than most folks learn in a lifetime. It was my culinary school before I knew there was such a thing.

It was there that I got my education on the art of buttermilk-brined and -battered fried chicken with a crackly crust that snapped at the first bite. I learned to make a crispy crust chicken pie so rich it sends your taste buds into overdrive. I discovered the art of a spicy shrimp and okra gumbo made by the hands of a talented Creole cook who could just as well have cooked in the hallowed kitchens of Galatoire's or Antoine's as my father's road-side diner.

Cutting biscuits was my job, and I learned never to twist the biscuit cutter, or the edges wouldn't rise. I discovered that even heat distribution of a well-seasoned cast-iron skillet was the secret to frying chicken. And I learned that salt, properly applied, brings out the vibrancy of flavor, even in the sweetest of dishes. It was an early education in down-home roots cooking that I packed up with me as I began my journey of discovery of the food of Louisiana.

COOKING MY WAY ALONG THE BAYOU BACK ROADS

As a young man, I left my hometown, and at every stop, I sopped up every bit of knowledge about the food culture of the people who lived there. That journey led me to Lafayette, Louisiana, where I explored the mystique of Cajun and Creole cooking in my first book, *Acadiana Table*. Now I intend to broaden my search for culinary truth as I return to my Louisiana roots in this book, *Fresh from Louisiana*.

But this is more than a cookbook. It is an exploration of my heritage and the recipes and methods I have discovered over a lifetime of eating my way across the bayou state. This book is a guide to the Louisiana I know and love. A place where front porches are for conversations and backyards for celebrations. The Louisiana that's plain, simple, and—most of all—welcoming.

This book is rooted in down-home food culture like a stovetop anchored by simmering black pots of gumbo, grits, greens, and speckled butterbeans. There will be unexpected turns on familiar dishes that lead to a place you never knew existed. It is that exploration that stokes the fire in my belly, and I hope that it will inspire my readers to rethink the recipes they know.

AT THE FORK IN THE ROAD

It's a love affair that borders obsession and has turned me into a culinary stalker. For me, traveling the back roads is an adventure. There's always a fork in the road where food swerves from the ordinary to the extraordinary, turns from run-of-the-mill to remarkable, okay to oh-my-goodness. I like to eat in the small-town diners to sample the weekday's specialty. You know it's been on the menu for decades, and in the pot for only hours, and then it's gone until the same time next week. And I like the stories behind the food; every table has a tale.

I've said for years now that the stories tell themselves, but that's only partly true. Stories of Cajun and Creole families and the food that fuels generations are personal stories that take cajoling conversation, prodding questions, and gentle probing for family secrets. It's hard work. But when a kitchen table fills with notebooks, handwritten recipes, and empty plates, and you know you've uncovered just one more tasty tidbit, it's worth it.

INSPIRING NEW RECIPES

For many living outside my world, Louisiana cooking is misinterpreted, misappropriated, and ultimately misunderstood. Some folks tend to think of our cuisine as one general foodway, but the truth is that it is divided along cultural, geographic, socioeconomic, and ethnic lines of distinction. And that's what makes it so interesting to explore, as exciting new influences have added to the mystique. The cultural influences that helped define early Louisiana cuisine continue with the introduction of Vietnamese fishing communities along the Gulf and the influx of Hispanic workers to help rebuild the coast after Hurricane Katrina.

In the pages of *Fresh from Louisiana*, you'll see traditional ingredients with new, head-turning twists on recipes using them. I plan to stretch your worldview of Louisiana cooking in a way that expands your palate and perceptions. I'll cut corners and take a shortcut but only if it gets me to my culinary destination in style. We'll take a side trip down memory lane and explore the history of Louisiana's colorful food culture, but we will always stay focused on inspiring new dishes.

PREPARE FOR THE UNEXPECTED

With *Fresh from Louisiana*, you'll see off-the-cuff commentary on recipes that define our food culture and how new dishes have elbowed their place at the table. There are small bites of culinary wisdom (or at least I think so) and belt-loosening stories of what makes our roots cooking so tasty. For the most part, Louisiana food uses humble, inexpensive ingredients. But the food in this cookbook is not what you may expect; it's my take on many classic dishes without regard to conventional thinking on the subject.

Your grandmother's meatloaf is redefined when draped with a weave of smoked bacon and brushed with a spicy Tabasco pepper jelly glaze. Mac and cheese is a tried-and-true, down-home Southern staple, but in these pages, it's infused with briny Gulf shrimp and smoky Cajun tasso for a spicy version that will test your adventurous spirit. You won't find foie gras on my menu, but you'll discover that a slice of white bread, a ripe Creole tomato, and a smear of mayo can be just as enlightening.

I love it all: the buttermilk biscuits slathered with mayhaw jelly, a white bean soup simmering in hambone-infused potlikker, or a black iron skillet of hot cornbread coming out of the oven.

Fresh from Louisiana is a love letter to my obsession, to my passion. Thank you for joining me on the journey; I hope you enjoy the ride.

CHAPTER 1
SPRING

I'M DRIVEN TO POETIC PROSE when I think about the first days of spring and a bowl of my wife Roxanne's pure vegetable soup—the ultimate comfort food. I call this soup "pure" because of her emphasis on fresh, locally grown vegetables with a keen focus on the purity and potential of this hearty dish. Just cupping your hands around a steaming bowl is enough to warm your soul, and with the first spoonful of the beefy broth, you feel nourished, enriched, loved. She is a passionate cook, and this springtime recipe is her generous expression of farm-to-table family cooking.

Growing up in the rural community of Jennings, Louisiana, Rox had access to farm-grown vegetables that gave her a palate for quality when it comes to the simplest of ingredients. From her grandfather Clodius Fontenot's farm just down the road in Hathaway, the family always had a steady supply of handpicked produce as well as freshly preserved or canned fruits and vegetables. She was taught that a pot of vegetable soup is a sensible way to use up an overstocked pantry, and the ingredients that go into this simple recipe depended on what is the ripest and at the peak of season.

When I ask her about the method for her Pure Vegetable Soup, she rattles off a rapid-fire sequence of instructions: Use what is fresh . . . brown the meat, but no oil . . . veg stock, not beef stock . . . and store-bought is okay because it's going to make its own beef stock with the browned beef . . . no Cajun seasoning, just salt and pepper only . . . no tomato sauce, just fresh diced Creole tomatoes . . . slice the vegetables large, and do not overcook . . . add the ingredients to the pot in stages . . . frozen peas, not canned because flash-frozen preserves freshness . . . use Irish (or what her grandmother referred to as "arsh" potatoes), which are nothing more than russet potatoes. And on and on.

During her explanation, it struck me that several generations of experience were at work here. My wife wasn't just making soup, she was channeling family traditions, cooking knowledge, instructional information that was passed down from her Mo Mo Eve, and her mother, Rosalie Waldrop. And this recipe will live on as our daughter Lauren stirs a pot of soup for her family one day. It is Pure Vegetable Soup. It is pure love.

PURE VEGETABLE SOUP

This farm-to-table recipe takes advantage of the freshest locally grown vegetables. The choice of ingredients is up to you; just ensure they are at the peak of season.

1½ pounds (680 g) beef stew meat, cut into 1-inch (2.5 cm) cubes

1 cup (160 g) roughly chopped yellow onion

1 cup (120 g) roughly chopped celery

1 cup (150 g) roughly chopped green bell pepper

6 cups (1.4 L) vegetable stock

1 ripe tomato, chopped

1 cup (120 g) roughly chopped carrots

1 large russet potato, peeled and cut into chunks

1 cup (120 g) roughly chopped zucchini

1 cup (120 g) roughly chopped yellow squash

1 cup (70 g) roughly chopped broccoli

1 cup (100 g) fresh green beans

1 cup (150 g) frozen green peas

Kosher salt and freshly ground black pepper

1. Lightly coat a large pot with nonstick spray and place over medium-high heat. Add the beef and sear the meat until it browns on all sides, 8 to 10 minutes. Add the onion, celery, and bell pepper and cook for 5 minutes longer.

2. Pour in the stock a little at a time and stir, scraping up all the browned bits from the bottom of the pot. Add the rest of the stock and the tomato. Lower the heat to a simmer and continue to cook for 30 minutes until the meat becomes tender.

3. Add the carrots and potatoes and simmer for another 20 minutes. Add the zucchini, yellow squash, broccoli, green beans, and peas and simmer for another 20 minutes. Add salt and pepper to taste. Turn off the heat and let the soup rest for 15 minutes before serving.

4. Ladle the soup into bowls and serve with saltine crackers and butter, or better yet, a black iron skillet of cornbread.

CRAWFISH BOIL CHOWDER

Louisiana crawfish, spicy seasoned onions, potatoes, corn on the cob, and smoked sausage are at the base of this recipe, but it's the crawfish stock and cream thickened with a blond roux that bring together this chowder magnificently. But I clearly understand that some of you do not have the luxury of attending a crawfish boil, and accessing these boiled ingredients may not be readily available. Not to worry. I have an easy recipe without leftovers, and the result is just as tasty. Serve with hot French bread.

1 cup (64 g) dry crawfish boil seasoning mix (see Sources, page 232)

4 medium yellow onions

6 small potatoes

2 links smoked pork sausage

6 ears frozen corn on the cob

2 tablespoons (30 g) unsalted butter, plus more if needed

¼ cup (30 g) unbleached all-purpose flour, plus more if needed

3 cups (720 ml) crawfish stock or seafood stock

1 cup (240 ml) heavy cream

8 ounces (227 g) Louisiana crawfish tail meat (see Sources, page 232)

Hot sauce

Kosher salt and freshly ground black pepper

4 whole crawfish, for garnish (optional; see Sources, page 232)

½ cup (50 g) diced green onion tops

1. Fill a large pot halfway with water, place over medium-high heat, and bring to a boil. Add the seasoning, onions, potatoes, and sausage to the water and boil until the potatoes are cooked through, about 15 minutes. Add the corn and cook for another 5 minutes. Drain the vegetables and sausage and let cool.

2. Remove any outer peel or stem ends from the cooked onions and chop into bite-size chunks. With a sharp knife, slice the corn from the cobs and discard the cobs. Slice the potatoes and sausage links into bite-size chunks.

3. In a cast-iron pot over medium heat, melt the butter and add the flour. Combine the flour into the butter and stir to make a blond roux, about 5 minutes. Add the stock and stir to combine. Add all of the vegetables and sausage. Add the cream and bring to a simmer. Continue cooking until the soup begins to thicken into a chowder consistency, about 30 minutes. If it is too thick, add more stock or water. If the chowder is not thick enough, make a beurre manié (a French technique for thickening a sauce) by combining 2 tablespoons (30 g) softened butter with 2 tablespoons (16 g) flour and add it to the pot to thicken.

4. Add the crawfish tail meat and simmer for another 10 minutes. Add hot sauce, salt, and pepper to taste. Serve in shallow bowls garnished with a whole boiled crawfish, if desired, and diced green onion tops.

MINI CRAWFISH PIES

At first bite, you taste the flaky golden brown piecrust that holds the rich treasure inside. And with the second bite, the spicy crawfish filling coats your taste buds with one delicious mouthful. Once more, and then it's gone. But the taste lingers as you grab another and another. Crawfish pie in a mini version is the perfect party food, before-dinner appetizer, or accompaniment to a side salad for a delicious lunch. Regardless of your dining objective, you will love both the taste and the ease of preparation of this recipe.

CRAWFISH FILLING

1 cup (240 g) unsalted butter

1 cup (160 g) finely diced yellow onion

1 teaspoon minced garlic

1 cup (120 g) all-purpose flour, divided

1 cup (240 ml) seafood stock

1 pound (455 g) Louisiana crawfish tail meat (see Sources, page 232)

½ cup (50 g) finely diced green onion tops

1 teaspoon paprika

1 teaspoon Cajun Seasoning Blend (page 231)

Kosher salt and freshly ground black pepper

Dash of hot sauce

CRAWFISH FILLING

1. In a large cast-iron pot or skillet over medium-high heat, melt the butter. Add the onion and sauté until translucent, about 5 minutes. Add the garlic, lower the heat to a simmer, and stir to combine. Sprinkle ½ cup (60 g) of the flour over the mixture, stir to incorporate, and cook the flour until it turns light brown, about 10 minutes. Add the stock, and stir until you reach a stew-like thickness.

2. Add the crawfish tail meat and green onion tops and simmer for 15 minutes. Add the paprika, Cajun seasoning, and season to taste with salt, pepper, and hot sauce. At this point, you want to thicken the mixture until it achieves the texture of a filling or stuffing by gradually stirring in the remaining ½ cup (60 g) flour. Bring the mixture back to a simmer and turn off the heat. Cover and refrigerate for a minimum of 1 hour or until ready to use.

PIECRUST

1 cup (120 g) all-purpose flour, plus more for sprinkling

2 (15 ounce [425 g]) piecrust packages (2 crusts in each), thawed to room temperature

1 large egg, beaten

Kosher salt

PIECRUST

1. Preheat the oven to 350°F (180°C). Have ready 12 3-inch (7.5 cm) pie tins.

2. Lightly sprinkle flour on a large countertop surface (granite or marble works well). Unwrap and unroll one of the piecrust sheets; sprinkle lightly with more flour. Using a rolling pin, roll until it spreads to a thickness of ¼ inch (6 mm). Using the top of your pie tin as a guide, cut a circle in the dough with a sharp knife, leaving enough of a border to form the edge of the crust. Repeat to cut out the remaining piecrusts. Place the dough into each pie tin and crimp the edges. Chill the crusts in the refrigerator for at least 1 hour or until ready to fill.

3. Spoon the crawfish filling into the center of each piecrust. Place the mini pies on a baking sheet lined with parchment. Repeat with all the pies.

4. At this point, you can refrigerate (or freeze) the pies until ready to bake. Right before baking, lightly brush the edge of the piecrust with the egg. Bake in the oven until golden brown, 20 to 30 minutes. Serve in a basket as an appetizer or as an accompaniment to a side salad.

NOTES For a circle guide, use your aluminum pie tin to trace out on a piece of paper a diameter larger than the top of your tin, then use this as a template. The size of your pie tin will determine the number of pies you can make. Try this recipe with small shrimp or crab for a tasty seafood variation. When refrigerated, the crawfish filling should be thick enough to form into a ball. Any extra crawfish filling makes the perfect stuffing for a breakfast omelette. I do not recommend reheating in the microwave; bake in the oven until heated through.

HOW TO EAT BOILED CRAWFISH

The crawfish season is in full swing, and no doubt, folks are coming to our state to belly up to a table full of boiled crawfish for the first time. As far as local culinary traditions go, eating boiled crawfish is a seasonal social outing that is second nature to anyone raised on the bayou. But there are lots of out-of-towners who are anxious to eat boiled crawfish for the very first time. And they all want to know in advance what the "rules of engagement" are for this mysterious culinary ritual. How to dress? How to prepare? How to keep from making a fool of yourself? These are good questions, and if you follow these five simple rules you will look, act, and peel like a local, not a yokel.

1. DRESS APPROPRIATELY

No fancy-schmancy Charleston seersucker, socialite, dressy duds. Dress down, not up. Jeans are perfectly fine. Don't wear a white shirt—the darker the better—and short sleeves are recommended. By the way, you may be offered a bib (yes, some waiters can recognize a newbie from across the room) and feel free to use it, as many experienced locals do. Although I've seen 300-pound oilfield roustabouts wearing bibs (usually with a picture of a lobster on it), I find it unnecessary. It's a personal thing. Besides, that's why I'm wearing the dark shirt. And for goodness' sake, take out your contact lenses and wear your glasses: the spice on your hands will linger no matter how many times you wash them.

2. BEER IN HAND

No wine. No sweet tea. No mojito-rita-tini frappe. Just an ice-cold bottle of beer. Or two. And if you're a teetotaler, opt for water, which you will need anyway.

3. THE ORDER OF THINGS

If at a backyard crawfish boil, the standing position along a long table covered with newspaper is the usual method. If eating crawfish for the first time in a restaurant, sit. Order the 5-pound (2.3 kg) tray (trust me, you'll want it all). Order it seasoned "mild"—remember, you are a first-timer; don't go kamikaze on me. "Mild" is boiled in seasoned water and is plenty hot to most neophytes, and I've seen a lot of brutes buckle under the pressure of a "spicy hot" mound of mudbugs. Anyway, you can always sprinkle on a little Cajun seasoning at the table. Ask for another beer.

4. THE ADD-ONS

Stick with tradition. Get the corn and potatoes, and especially the onions (they are not like any onions you've ever eaten—spicy, yet sweet). Pass on the trendy mushrooms, artichokes, sausage links, and any other add-on *du jour* taking up room in the boiling pot (and your stomach). Sauce is optional, but if you're a "dunker," make your own dipping sauce—ketchup, mayo, horseradish, Worcestershire, lemon juice, and hot sauce—in any

varying intensity that strikes your fancy. Order another beer.

5. THE STEAMING HOT TRAY

With a mountain of screaming-hot, just-out-of-the-pot boiled crawfish sitting right in front of you, you are now in uncharted waters. As you take a whiff and your sinuses open up, it's time to wipe the fog from your glasses and survey the massive mound of steaming mudbugs in front of you. Your first primal instinct is fear of the unknown. Don't panic. Don't run. Resist any inner urge to scream for help. Roll up your sleeves and take a long drink of ice-cold beer.

Don't even think about asking someone to peel your crawfish for you. The bayou rule is "you've got to peel your crawfish bayou self." Look around the restaurant, and you'll even see five-year-old kids peeling their own; it is a Cajun rite of passage.

Survey your tray of crawfish; it's okay if the sizes vary, but they should all look uniform in color (red) with curled tails. Old-school locals swear that a straight-tail crawfish is dead before it is cooked, but that is debatable. I always listen to experience and suggest removing and discarding them anyway.

Tackle the tray head-on. Align your sauce bowl to one side and your shell basket to the other. Take

the first crawfish with the tail in your left hand and the head in your right. Break off the head and in one motion bring it to your waiting mouth and squeeze. Sucking the head juices spiked with crawfish fat and spicy seasoning is a ceremonial entry into the Cajun world. With that one act of legitimacy, you have now removed any trace of being a tourist and have firmly established yourself as a crawfish-eating local.

Next, you have several tail-peeling options. First up is the impressively skillful, one-handed bite-pull-and-pinch technique that you will see many seasoned Cajuns use. Even I haven't mastered this one, so let's move on to more manageable methods for getting the tail meat out of the shell. My wife subscribes to the two-thumbs technique of splitting open the tail down the middle and lifting out the meat. I am more methodical: Hold the tail in your right hand and with your left hand, peel the

first and second rings of shell from the tail while squeezing the bottom of the tail with the thumb of your right hand. This pinching action will free the tail meat. Take a quick look at it and remove any black vein (similar to a shrimp) along the back of the tail. You can now dunk it into your bowl of dipping sauce and devour. Take a swig of beer and repeat about fifty more times.

Watch the repetitive action of others around you and find your rhythm—your peeling pace. And have fun; it's a party. As crawfish juices run down your arms (you should have worn short sleeves) and your tongue tingles from the peppery heat, you will be overcome with a sense of joy and understanding of how delightfully delicious this culturally significant culinary ritual is. And you will feel victorious in your accomplishment.

Congratulations. You are now a bona fide, head-suckin', tail-pinchin', boiled crawfish expert.

CORN AND CRAB BISQUE

This cream-based soup has its origins in the Creole culinary culture of New Orleans, but these days you're just as likely to find it on the stovetop in home kitchens across the state. It is a marriage made in Cajun and Creole heaven. Serve with hot French bread.

INGREDIENTS

6 strips smoked bacon, chopped

1 cup (160 g) diced yellow onion

1 cup (120 g) diced celery

1 cup (150 g) diced bell pepper

1 tablespoon (15 g) unsalted butter

1 tablespoon (8 g) all-purpose flour

1 tablespoon (8 g) Cajun Seasoning Blend (page 231)

1 tablespoon (15 ml) hot sauce

4 cups (960 ml) half-and-half

½ cup (120 ml) sherry

2 cups (300 g) fresh-cut or canned corn

1 pound (455 g) fresh Louisiana white lump crabmeat (see Sources, page 232)

1 tablespoon (3 g) chopped fresh thyme

2 tablespoons (6 g) fresh chopped flat-leaf parsley

Kosher salt and freshly ground black pepper

1 cup (100 g) diced green onion tops

1. In a large black iron pot over medium-high heat, add the bacon pieces. Cook until the bacon is browned, about 8 minutes, and then remove to a paper towel to drain. Reserve for later use.

2. Pour off all but 1 tablespoon (15 ml) of the bacon grease and return to medium-high heat. Add the onion, celery, and bell pepper and cook until browned, about 5 minutes. Decrease the heat to low and add the butter and flour to the vegetable mixture. Whisk the flour rapidly until it blends into the butter and begins to cook, about 2 minutes. Add the Cajun seasoning and hot sauce and stir to combine. Add the half-and-half and sherry and stir to combine. Add the corn, crabmeat, thyme, and parsley. Stir and simmer for 20 minutes until thickened to a bisque-like consistency.

3. Taste the bisque and add salt and pepper along with more hot sauce if needed.

4. Ladle into bowls and garnish with a sprinkling of green onion tops and the reserved bacon pieces.

EGGS AND BOUDIN

For my money, you can put a perfectly fried egg atop just about anything and I'd eat it. But crown a spicy patty made of Cajun boudin, and we're talking the goose (uh, chicken) that laid the golden egg. In South Louisiana, combining eggs and boudin is a rural Cajun recipe for breakfast. Hearty country Cajun breakfasts are well known, and boudin frequently competes for center of the plate with farm-fresh eggs. Yep, boudin is the perfect nest for my egg, and if you've never had this combination, then you're in luck.

BISCUITS

2 cups (240 g) self-rising flour, plus more for sprinkling

½ cup (120 ml) buttermilk

½ cup (120 g) mayonnaise

2 tablespoons (30 g) unsalted butter, at room temperature, divided

BISCUITS

1. Preheat the oven to 450°F (230°C). Line a baking sheet with parchment paper.

2. In a large mixing bowl, sift the flour. In a separate bowl, add the buttermilk and whisk in the mayonnaise and 1 tablespoon (15 g) of the softened butter. Make a well in the center of the flour and add the liquid. Using a spoon, slowly incorporate the flour into the wet ingredients by folding it over. Continue until it comes together.

3. Pour the contents of the bowl onto a work surface sprinkled with more flour. If the dough is too wet, add a little more flour. Using your hands, gently bring the mixture together and pat it down into a ½-inch (1.3 cm)-thick rectangle. Fold the dough over onto itself and pat down once again. Repeat this one more time and pat it to ½ inch (1.3 cm) thick.

4. Using a 3-inch (7.5 cm)-diameter biscuit cutter, cut out 4 biscuit rounds and move them to the prepared baking sheet. Place the biscuits in the oven and bake until golden brown, 15 to 20 minutes. Remove from the oven, split open, and brush with the remaining 1 tablespoon (15 g) butter. Keep warm until serving.

BACON AND EGGS

1 pound (455 g) smoked bacon

2 pounds (910 g) Cajun boudin, homemade (page 229) or store-bought (see Sources, page 232), removed from casings

4 large eggs

¼ cup (25 g) diced green onion tops

Kosher salt and freshly ground black pepper

Pinch of Cajun Seasoning Blend (page 231)

BACON AND EGGS

1. In a large skillet over medium-high heat, add the strips of bacon and cook until crispy. Turn off the heat, remove the bacon, drain on paper towels, and reserve for later. Pour off all but 2 tablespoons (30 ml) of the bacon fat and return the skillet to the stovetop.

2. Shape the boudin into four 3-inch (7.5 cm)-diameter patties about 1 inch (2.5 cm) thick.

3. On four plates, add the bottom half of a biscuit, top each with 2 strips of crispy bacon, and add a warm boudin patty on top.

4. When your guests are seated, turn the burner under the skillet to medium. Crack the eggs into a small bowl and add to the pan. Fry the eggs until they reach your desired doneness. With a spatula, transfer the fried eggs from the grease directly onto each plated boudin patty, being careful not to break the yolk. Sprinkle with the diced green onion tops and season the eggs with salt, pepper, and a pinch of Cajun seasoning.

CRAWFISH OMELETTE

Cracking a trio of farm-fresh eggs is just the start of making this omelette. I like the artistry of using eggs as my canvas in layering the colors and flavors of fresh herbs and aromatics, with plump crawfish tails punctuating the dish for a cultural twist. Served open-face, this dish redefines the art of the omelette. And if the omelette is to be thought of as the definitive French dish, then let this version define my French Louisiana culinary roots. *C'est bon!*

3 tablespoons (45 g) unsalted butter, divided

Tail meat of 12 precooked crawfish, thawed if frozen (see Sources, page 232)

2 tablespoons (20 g) finely diced green onion

1 tablespoon (10 g) finely diced yellow onion

1 teaspoon minced garlic

1 tablespoon (16 g) finely minced red sweet mini pepper

Leaves of 1 thyme sprig

2 tablespoons (6 g) chopped flat-leaf parsley

3 large eggs

1 teaspoon Cajun Seasoning Blend (page 231)

Sea salt

1 whole crawfish (optional), for garnish (see Sources, page 232)

1. Preheat the oven to 200°F (93°C).

2. In a 9-inch (23 cm) nonstick pan over medium heat, add 1 tablespoon (15 g) of the butter. Once sizzling hot, add the crawfish tails and cook until just warmed through, about 1 minute. Drain on a paper towel and keep warm.

3. In the same pan over medium heat, add 1 tablespoon (15 g) of the butter. Once sizzling hot, add the onions, garlic, pepper, thyme, and parsley. Cook just until the yellow onion turns translucent, about 3 minutes. Remove to a platter and keep warm.

4. In the same pan over medium heat, add the remaining 1 tablespoon (15 g) butter.

5. Crack the eggs into a bowl and add the Cajun seasoning. Whisk until beaten. Once the butter is sizzling, swirl it around in the pan to cover the entire surface. Add the eggs to the pan and, with a rubber spatula, stir the eggs. Continue stirring until the eggs just begin to set, and then smooth them out to cover the bottom of the pan.

6. Add the cooked aromatics and herbs evenly across the eggs, and distribute the crawfish tails on top of that. Place the pan in the warm oven to heat through all the ingredients, about 5 minutes.

7. Remove from the oven and, using the spatula, gently slide the omelette from the pan and onto a warm plate. Sprinkle with sea salt and garnish with a whole crawfish in the center (if you have it). Serve immediately while hot.

PREP TIME: 45 MINUTES
COOK TIME: 40 MINUTES
TOTAL TIME: 1 HOUR 25 MINUTES

EGGPLANT CASSEROLE WITH GULF SHRIMP

With fresh, farm-to-table eggplant infused with meaty pork sausage and aromatic herbs and vegetables, this dressing is the perfect backdrop for briny Gulf shrimp. I love how it all combines with Louisiana rice in a casserole that bakes up delicious every time.

1 tablespoon (15 ml) bacon grease

1 cup (160 g) diced yellow onion

1 cup (150 g) diced green bell pepper

1 cup (120 g) diced celery

1 pound (455 g) raw pork sausage, such as Cajun green onion sausage (see Sources, page 232)

2 large eggplants, peeled and cubed

1 tablespoon (8 g) minced garlic

1 tablespoon (3 g) finely chopped fresh rosemary

2 tablespoons (6 g) chopped flat-leaf parsley

1 cup (200 g) cooked long-grain white rice

½ cup (120 ml) dark chicken stock

1 teaspoon browning sauce, such as Kitchen Bouquet

1½ teaspoons Cajun Seasoning Blend (page 231)

Kosher salt and freshly ground black pepper

1 pound (455 g) jumbo (16/20 count) shrimp, peeled and deveined

1. Preheat the oven to 350°F (180°C). Coat a 9 x 13-inch (23 x 33 cm) ovenproof casserole dish with nonstick spray.

2. In a large pot over medium-high heat, add the bacon grease. Add the onion, bell pepper, and celery, and cook until the onions turn translucent. Add the sausage and cook until browned, about 8 minutes. Add the eggplant and continue cooking until the eggplant softens, about 5 minutes. Stir in the garlic, rosemary, parsley, and cooked rice. Add the chicken stock and browning sauce and lower the heat to a simmer. Cook for 10 minutes until the stock is absorbed.

3. Season with the Cajun seasoning and taste the mixture, adjusting with salt and black pepper as needed. Turn off the heat and let the mixture rest until ready to bake.

4. Add the mixture to the prepared casserole dish, arranging the shrimp on top. Bake uncovered for 20 minutes until warmed through and the shrimp turn pink. Remove from the oven and serve family style.

NOTES When a dish calls for a dark, rich color (like this one), I always add a dash or two of Kitchen Bouquet. The shrimp can be substituted with crabmeat or crawfish tails for other tasty versions.

EGGPLANT—VEGETABLE OR FRUIT?

Yes, I refer to eggplant as a vegetable, as most of you do. However, a bit of research reveals that it is indeed a fruit. It is an odd ingredient in every way. Almost inedible in its raw state, it is bitter with an unpleasant spongy texture. However, once it is sautéed and the sponge-like eggplant begins absorbing the flavors and liquids around it, it becomes magical. The everyday supermarket purple eggplant, the yellow variety, or the Italian Rosa Bianca—they're all good. And when I see them, I always load up. Baked, stuffed, roasted, stewed, fried, or in a casserole, eggplant can't be beaten.

FARMERS' MARKET SALAD WITH BLOOD ORANGE VINAIGRETTE

Spring is in full swing, and around the Graham house, we tend to eat light. Sometimes Rox and I will fix an entire dinner and never even fire up the stove or grill. Eating raw off the land is a treat for us, and this salad is a revelation—the perfect expression of farm-to-plate freshness. I love the earthy flavors, the crunch of uncooked vegetables, and the sweet kiss from the blood orange dressing.

VINAIGRETTE

¼ cup (60 ml) blood orange juice

1 tablespoon (15 ml) white wine vinegar

1 teaspoon lemon juice

1 teaspoon Creole mustard or coarse-grained mustard

About ¾ cup (180 ml) extra-virgin olive oil

Kosher salt and freshly ground black pepper

SALAD

3 large red beets, peeled and spiralized

Kosher salt and freshly ground black pepper

2 heads red leaf lettuce

1 bunch red kale

2 bunches carrots, peeled

1 bunch assorted radishes, thinly sliced

2 large red onions, sliced

3 blood oranges, peeled and sliced

8 ripe strawberries, hulled and halved

6 small tomatoes

2 cups (120 g) fresh basil leaves

4 stalks green onion

VINAIGRETTE

1. In a small mixing bowl, add the orange juice, vinegar, lemon juice, and mustard. While whisking, drizzle enough olive oil, about ¾ cup, into the bowl until it begins to emulsify. Season to taste with salt and pepper. Cover and refrigerate.

SALAD

1. Place the spiralized beets in a non-metallic bowl. Pour over the vinaigrette and toss. Refrigerate for 2 hours or up to 2 days ahead.

2. On each of four large plates, add a base of red leaf lettuce and kale. Remove the bowl containing the beets and strain off the vinaigrette into a serving bowl. Add the beets to the plates. Place portions of the carrots, radishes, red onion, orange slices, strawberries, and tomatoes on each of the salads. Add the basil and green onion. Sprinkle with salt and a grind of pepper.

3. Chill the salads in the refrigerator for 30 minutes before serving. Serve with the dressing and more freshly ground pepper on the side.

NOTES Venture to your farmers' market and get creative with your salad ingredients; add what you like, but be sure to buy the freshest locally grown produce. Buy a spiralizer and open up a whole new world of eating fresh vegetables. Be sure to wear disposable gloves (or wash your hands immediately) when peeling and spiralizing red beets.

CRAB-STUFFED PORTOBELLO

The large, round portobello mushrooms I see at the farmers' markets are just begging to be stuffed and are just the right size for a creamy, cheesy seafood and herb-infused blend of flavors. This dish is perfect for a light lunch or an evening meal paired with a green salad lightly dressed with your choice of dressing and a bottle of chilled white wine.

5 large portobello mushrooms

½ cup (120 g) unsalted butter

½ cup (80 g) diced yellow onion

½ cup (60 g) diced celery

1 tablespoon (8 g) minced garlic

½ cup (120 ml) dry vermouth or dry white wine (optional)

1 cup (60 g) chopped fresh basil

1 tablespoon (3 g) chopped fresh thyme, plus 4 sprigs, for garnish

1 teaspoon smoked paprika

Kosher salt and freshly ground black pepper

Dash of hot sauce

8 ounces (227 g) Louisiana lump crabmeat (see Sources, page 232)

2 tablespoons (10 g) grated Parmesan cheese

1 cup (100 g) fresh unseasoned bread crumbs

2 cups (240 g) grated Monterey Jack cheese

2 tablespoons (30 ml) extra-virgin olive oil

1. Preheat the oven to 350°F (180°C). Line a baking sheet with parchment paper.

2. Using a scrub brush, clean the tops of the mushrooms. With a teaspoon, remove the stem and scrape out the dark brown gills inside. Chop one of the mushrooms for later use. Transfer the remaining whole mushrooms to the prepared baking sheet and set aside.

3. In a large skillet over medium heat, melt the butter. Add the onion, celery, and chopped mushroom and cook until the onions turn translucent, about 5 minutes. Add the garlic and vermouth (if using). Cook until the liquor begins to burn off and the vermouth reduces by half, about 5 minutes. Add the basil and thyme. Turn off the heat.

4. Season to taste with the paprika, salt, pepper, and hot sauce. Add the crabmeat and grated Parmesan. At this point, the mixture should have significant moisture to add the bread crumbs. Stir in the bread crumbs and distribute evenly throughout the mixture until absorbed.

5. Spoon the stuffing mixture inside each mushroom. Top with a generous sprinkling of the Monterey Jack and a drizzle of the olive oil. Place in the oven and cook for approximately 15 minutes until the cheese begins to bubble and turn brown. Remove from the oven and keep warm.

6. To serve, place one stuffed mushroom on a plate and garnish with a sprig of thyme.

SHRIMP AND TASSO MAC AND CHEESE WITH CRACKLIN' CRUST

Shrimp and tasso are a common combination in my Louisiana cooking bag of tricks; the smoky, spicy sausage infuses flavor into the briny Gulf shellfish. It all blends beautifully with the savory depth of mushrooms, and two creamy cheeses cloak the ingredients with a rich, velvety robe of flavor. And to top it all off, I'm adding a crust of crunchy pork cracklins as the "spicing on the cake."

1 (16-ounce [455 g]) package elbow macaroni

2 tablespoons (30 g) unsalted butter

½ cup (80 g) diced yellow onion

½ cup (60 g) diced celery

½ cup (75 g) diced green bell pepper

1 cup (75 g) chopped mushrooms (button or portobello)

1 cup (150 g) chopped tasso or smoked ham (see Sources, page 232)

1 tablespoon (8 g) all-purpose flour

2 cups (480 ml) whole milk

1 cup (240 ml) heavy cream

2 cups (240 g) shredded Cheddar cheese

1 cup (120 g) shredded fontina cheese

1 teaspoon white pepper

1 teaspoon hot sauce

Kosher salt

1 pound (455 g) jumbo (16/20 count) shrimp, peeled and deveined

1 cup (75 g) crushed pork cracklins or pork rinds (see Sources, page 232)

1. Preheat the oven to 350°F (180°C).

2. Bring a large pot of water to a boil over high heat. Add the macaroni and cook according to the package directions. Strain the pasta and keep warm for later use.

3. In a large cast-iron skillet over medium-high heat, add the butter. Once the butter is sizzling, add the onion, celery, bell pepper, mushrooms, and tasso. Cook until the onions turn translucent and the mushrooms and tasso just begin to brown, about 8 minutes.

4. Sprinkle the mixture with the flour, and add the milk and cream. Bring to a boil and lower the heat to a simmer.

5. Add the cheeses and season with the white pepper, hot sauce, and a pinch of salt to taste. Add the cooked macaroni to the skillet and stir into the mixture.

6. Once the mixture thickens, add the shrimp, distributing them evenly throughout the skillet.

7. Sprinkle over the crushed pork cracklins and move the skillet to the hot oven.

8. Bake just until the mixture begins to bubble and the top begins to brown, about 10 minutes. Remove from the oven and serve immediately.

NOTE If you cannot source pork cracklins or pork skins, use one cup of panko bread crumbs spiced with 1 tablespoon (7 g) Cajun seasoning combined with 2 tablespoons (30 g) melted butter as your topping.

MINI BELL PEPPERS STUFFED WITH CRABMEAT

These little bell peppers with a light crabmeat stuffing are bursting with flavor. It's easy and elegant; this dish is the perfect light lunch or a first course at dinner.

RÉMOULADE SAUCE

½ cup (120 g) mayonnaise

½ cup (90 g) Creole mustard or coarse-grained mustard

1 tablespoon (10 g) finely diced yellow onion

2 tablespoons (16 g) finely diced celery

1 tablespoon (3 g) chopped flat-leaf parsley

1 teaspoon minced garlic

1 teaspoon lemon juice

½ teaspoon Cajun Seasoning Blend (page 231)

Dash of hot sauce

STUFFED PEPPERS

4 small bell peppers

1 pound (455 g) white lump crabmeat (see Sources, page 232)

¼ cup (30 g) finely diced celery

3 tablespoons (30 g) finely diced red onion

2 tablespoons (6 g) chopped flat-leaf parsley

2 tablespoons (30gl) mayonnaise

½ teaspoon Cajun Seasoning Blend (page 231)

1 large egg

½ cup (50 g) panko bread crumbs

4 lemon wedges

RÉMOULADE SAUCE

1. In a mixing bowl, whisk together the mayonnaise and mustard. Add the onion, celery, parsley, and garlic; stir to combine. Stir in the lemon juice, Cajun seasoning, and hot sauce. Cover and chill for at least an hour to let the flavors meld.

STUFFED PEPPERS

1. Preheat the oven to 350°F (180°C). Line a baking dish with parchment paper.

2. Wash the peppers and, with a sharp knife, slice the top off each pepper, reserving the tops. With a small spoon, scrape out the membranes and remove any seeds. Bring a large pot filled halfway with water to a boil over high heat. Add the peppers and submerge them below the water line and blanch just until tender, about 5 minutes. Remove and drain on paper towels.

3. Place the crabmeat in a glass mixing bowl and inspect to make sure all shells and cartilage are removed.

4. In another mixing bowl, add the celery, onion, and parsley. Add the mayonnaise and Cajun seasoning. Crack the egg into the mixture and add the bread crumbs. With a fork, mix until combined.

5. Add the crabmeat to the mixture and gently fold in the crabmeat to distribute evenly, but not enough to break up the lumps. Cover and chill until ready to stuff the peppers.

6. Spoon the stuffing into each pepper and place in the prepared baking dish. Place in the hot oven and bake just until the stuffing sets and the tops begin to brown, about 30 minutes.

7. To serve, move the stuffed peppers to a platter and dollop with one spoonful of the sauce. Garnish with the tops of the peppers and fresh lemon wedges. Serve the remaining sauce on the side.

SHRIMP AND ZUCCHINI PIROGUE

My pirogue features zucchini hollowed out and fried as a vessel for fresh, briny Gulf jumbo shrimp. Stewed down in a spicy étouffée and fried up golden brown, these shrimp deliver a contrast of texture and a boatload of flavor.

SHRIMP ÉTOUFFÉE

½ cup (120 g) plus 1 tablespoon (15 g) unsalted butter, divided

1 cup (160 g) diced yellow onion

1 cup (150 g) diced green bell pepper

1 cup (120 g) diced celery

1 tablespoon (8 g) minced garlic

2 tablespoons (16 g) unbleached all-purpose flour

1 cup (240 ml) seafood stock

1 tablespoon (15 g) tomato paste

1 pound (455 g) jumbo (16/20 count) shrimp, peeled, tail off, and deveined

1 teaspoon cayenne pepper

Kosher salt and freshly ground black pepper

Dash of hot sauce

¼ cup (12 g) chopped flat-leaf parsley

SHRIMP ÉTOUFFÉE

1. In a large cast-iron pot or skillet over medium-high heat, melt ½ cup (120 g) of the butter and add the onion, bell pepper, and celery. Sauté until the onions turn translucent, about 5 minutes. Add the garlic, lower the heat to a simmer, and stir to combine. Sprinkle the flour over the mixture, stir to incorporate, and cook the flour until it turns light brown, about 10 minutes. Add the stock and tomato paste, and stir until you reach a stew-like thickness.

2. Add the shrimp; stir the mixture to combine. Simmer the shrimp until they cook through and turn pink, about 10 minutes. Season to taste with the cayenne, salt, pepper, and hot sauce. As a final touch, stir in the remaining 1 tablespoon (15 g) butter along with the chopped parsley. Bring the étouffée back to a simmer and turn off the heat.

FRIED SHRIMP

1. In a pot or skillet over medium-high heat, add the oil and bring to a temperature of 375°F (190°C).

2. In a mixing bowl, beat the eggs and add the shrimp.

3. In a separate mixing bowl, combine the cornmeal, flour, and dry seasoning. Add the shrimp and coat them evenly.

4. Add the shrimp to the oil and fry until golden brown, 3 to 5 minutes. Remove and drain on paper towels. Sprinkle lightly with salt.

recipe continues

FRIED SHRIMP

4 cups (960 ml) canola oil, for frying

2 large eggs

12 colossal (8/10 count) shrimp, peeled, tail on, and deveined

2 cups (240 g) cornmeal

1 cup (120 g) unbleached all-purpose flour

2 tablespoons (16 g) Cajun Seasoning Blend (page 231)

Kosher salt

ZUCCHINI PIROGUE AND FRIES

6 large zucchini, divided

2 tablespoons (16 g) Cajun Seasoning Blend (page 231)

4 large eggs, beaten

2 cups (240 g) unbleached all-purpose flour

1 gallon (3.6 L) canola oil, for frying

Kosher salt

4 cups (800 g) cooked long-grain white rice

4 lemon wedges

1 cup (100 g) diced green onion tops

ZUCCHINI PIROGUE AND FRIES

1. With a sharp knife, slice off a thin layer lengthwise along the side of 4 of the zucchini, exposing the flesh of the squash. With a teaspoon, scoop out the flesh without penetrating the sides or bottom of the zucchini "boat." Reserve the scooped-out flesh for later use.

2. Slice the remaining 2 zucchini by trimming off the ends and cutting them in half through the center. Slice lengthwise until you have thick fry-shaped spears. Sprinkle the raw zucchini fries as well as the inside of each zucchini pirogue with a light dusting of the Cajun seasoning.

3. In a mixing bowl, add the beaten eggs.

4. In another mixing bowl, add the flour.

5. In a large pot over medium-high heat, add the oil and bring to a temperature of 375°F (190°C).

6. Dip the zucchini pirogues in the egg wash and coat with egg on the inside as well as the outer peel. Immediately roll in the flour and add to the hot oil. Fry until the zucchini are golden brown, about 10 minutes. Place on a wire rack with the hollow side facing down to allow any grease to drain. Sprinkle lightly with salt.

7. Add the reserved zucchini flesh along with the fries to the beaten egg. Immediately roll in the flour and add to the hot oil. Fry until golden brown, 5 to 8 minutes. Drain on a wire rack and salt immediately.

8. To assemble, place a zucchini pirogue on a plate and add a scoop of rice to the center of the "boat." Spoon over a generous portion of shrimp étouffée and top with 3 fried shrimp. Add a few zucchini fries and garnish with a slice of lemon and a sprinkle of green onion tops.

❧ PIROGUE ❧

The term *pirogue* has a dual meaning in South Louisiana. French for "boat," a pirogue is a legendary canoe-like vessel that was a common mode of transportation in the early days of Cajun life. Paddling along the tranquil bayous, these slim, shallow boats were hand-carved by artisans, and the craft still exists to this day. But in my culinary world, a pirogue is a vessel of a different sort.

GULF SHRIMP PASTA PRIMAVERA

Translated from Italian, *primavera* means "spring." And in my Cajun recipe book, there is no dish that combines light, refreshing spring flavors like this one. With garden-fresh vegetables kissed with sweet leaves of basil, all tied together with a pungent olive oil–infused bucatini pasta, the only thing that could elevate this to Louisiana recipe standards is the addition of the freshest seafood from coastal Gulf waters.

PASTA

2 tablespoons (36 g) salt

1 (16-ounce [455 g]) package thick pasta, such as bucatini or spaghetti

2 tablespoons (30 ml) olive oil

SHRIMP

24 jumbo (16/20 count) shrimp, peeled and deveined

1 tablespoon (8 g) Cajun Seasoning Blend (page 231)

2 tablespoons (30 ml) olive oil

2 tablespoons (16 g) minced garlic

VINAIGRETTE

1 teaspoon minced garlic

1 tablespoon (11 g) Dijon mustard

2 tablespoons (30 ml) freshly squeezed lemon juice

2 tablespoons (30 ml) red wine vinegar

½ teaspoon sugar

1 cup (240 ml) extra-virgin olive oil

Kosher salt and freshly ground black pepper

PASTA

1. Fill a large pot halfway with water and add the salt. Bring to a boil over high heat. Once the water is boiling, add the pasta and cook until al dente, about 15 minutes. Drain the water. Rinse the excess starch off the pasta and let drain. Toss with the olive oil; return the pasta to the dried pot and keep warm.

SHRIMP

1. Lightly sprinkle the shrimp on both sides with the Cajun seasoning.

2. In a skillet over medium-high heat, add the olive oil. Once sizzling hot, add the garlic and the shrimp. Sauté the shrimp just until the flesh turns slightly opaque and the exterior turns pink, about 3 minutes. Once done, remove to a platter and keep warm.

VINAIGRETTE

1. In a stainless steel mixing bowl, add the garlic, mustard, lemon juice, vinegar, and sugar. While slowly drizzling the olive oil, whisk together to make an emulsion. Season to taste with salt and pepper. Reserve for later use.

recipe continues

PRIMAVERA

1 cup (120 g) chopped celery

2 cups (300 g) julienned red bell pepper, seeds removed

1 large carrot, peeled and sliced or julienned

1 cup (160 g) thinly sliced red onion

1 cup (30 g) loosely packed fresh flat-leaf parsley, stems removed

4 cups (240 g) loosely packed fresh basil, stems removed, plus more for garnish

2 cups (300 g) multicolored cherry tomatoes, halved

1 medium zucchini, peeled and thinly sliced

1 medium yellow squash, peeled and thinly sliced

1 cup (100 g) diced green onion tops

1 tablespoon (5 g) red pepper flakes

2 tablespoons (2 g) dried Italian seasoning

2 tablespoons (16 g) freshly ground black pepper

½ lemon

1 cup (100 g) freshly grated Parmigiano-Reggiano cheese

Extra-virgin olive oil

PRIMAVERA

1. Move the pot with the pasta noodles to the stovetop over low heat. Add all the celery, pepper, carrot, onion, parsley, basil, tomatoes, zucchini, squash, and green onion to the pot. Using tongs, begin rotating the pasta with the mixture and incorporating all the ingredients. Add the shrimp and the vinaigrette. Stir to thoroughly coat the pasta with the vinaigrette. As the mixture begins to warm through, add the red pepper flakes, Italian seasoning, and black pepper. (Note: You are not cooking the ingredients but simply warming them through to serving temperature and enough to slightly wilt the vegetables.)

2. Remove the pot from the stovetop and squeeze in the lemon juice, being careful to catch any seeds. Add the cheese and stir to incorporate.

3. Keep warm for serving and at the last minute drizzle lightly with more olive oil. Serve in large bowls and garnish with more fresh basil leaves.

RABBIT GUMBO

When it comes to Louisiana roots cooking, this recipe is as deep-rooted as it gets. I love how the spicy flavors mingle with the rich meat of rabbit to create a gumbo that will humble even the most experienced Cajun cook. It is an exceptional and memorable dish. So, what could be better than a steaming bowl of rabbit gumbo? The second bowl.

¼ cup (60 ml) vegetable oil

1 cup (160 g) diced yellow onion

1 cup (150 g) diced green bell pepper

½ cup (75 g) diced red bell pepper

1 cup (120 g) diced celery

1 cup (150 g) diced tasso or smoked ham (see Sources, page 232)

3 cups (450 g) smoked pork sausage, cut crosswise into bite-size pieces

½ cup (25 g) chopped flat-leaf parsley

2 tablespoons (16 g) minced garlic

4 sprigs fresh rosemary

1¼ cups (300 ml) Dark Cajun Roux (page 230)

10 cups (2.4 L) dark chicken stock

1 teaspoon cayenne pepper

Hot sauce

Kosher salt and freshly ground black pepper

2 whole rabbits, cut into large pieces (see Sources, page 232)

8 cups (1.6 kg) cooked Louisiana long-grain white rice

Filé powder

1. In a large cast-iron pot with a lid over medium-high heat, add the oil. Add the onion, bell peppers, and celery and sauté until tender, about 5 minutes. Add the tasso or smoked ham and the sausage and continue to sauté. Add the parsley, garlic, and rosemary and stir to combine. Add the roux and dark chicken stock and stir to combine. Season with the cayenne and a dash of hot sauce. Lower the heat to a simmer, cover, and let cook for 30 minutes.

2. Uncover and taste the gumbo, adding salt and pepper to taste. Add the rabbit pieces. Cover and let simmer for 2 hours longer.

3. The roux will make this gumbo thick and rich, but not like a stew. If it is too thick, add more stock or water to thin it out to a bisque-like consistency. Remove the rosemary stems, sample the gumbo, and correct the seasoning to taste.

4. Serve the gumbo over rice with a sprinkling of filé powder.

ROX'S ROUX

Everyone should learn to make a roux. And once you've mastered the art of the roux, we have it all for your convenience in a jarred product we call Rox's Roux (see Sources, page 232). Made to my wife Roxanne's strictest formula, it is the deepest, darkest, and richest commercially available Cajun roux. The convenience of this product will add consistency and quality to any Louisiana roux-based recipe.

CAJUN RICE BOWL WITH GRIDDLED SHRIMP

So, how can I construct a healthy Louisiana recipe that doesn't skimp on the flavor and spice of down-home ingredients that I've come to know and love? Starting with shredded iceberg lettuce and the Cajun trinity—onion, celery, and bell pepper—lays a tasty foundation. Roasting little cubes of Louisiana sweet potatoes in a flavorful spice rub is a cinch. The spice-coated, roasted Louisiana pecans add crunch. Combining brown rice with Cajun-seasoned griddled shrimp provides an over-the-top presentation. And just to top it all off, why not garnish this Cajun rice bowl with spicy ribbons of carrot and fresh-picked flat-leaf parsley from the garden?

2 cups (300 g) diced sweet potato

6 tablespoons (90 ml) extra-virgin olive oil, divided, plus more for drizzling

¼ cup (30 g) Sweet Heat Seasoning (page 231)

1 cup (140 g) pecan halves

1½ tablespoons (8 g) Cajun Seasoning Blend (page 231), divided

1 large carrot

8 jumbo (16/20 count) shrimp, peeled, deveined, tail on

½ cup (80 g) diced yellow onion

½ cup (75 g) diced red bell pepper

½ cup (75 g) chopped green bell pepper

½ cup (60 g) diced celery

4 cups (800 g) cooked brown rice

½ cup (50 g) slivered green onion tops

½ cup (55 g) shredded carrot

4 cups (120 g) shredded iceberg lettuce

2 small bunches fresh flat-leaf parsley

2 tablespoons (30 ml) lemon juice, divided

Kosher salt and coarsely ground black pepper

1. Preheat the oven to 350°F (180°C). Line two baking sheets with foil.

2. In a mixing bowl, add the sweet potatoes along with 1 tablespoon (15 ml) of the olive oil. Turn to coat them evenly and sprinkle lightly with the Sweet Heat Seasoning. Spread out the sweet potatoes on one of the prepared baking sheets, and roast in the oven until tender, about 30 minutes. Keep warm until serving.

3. In a mixing bowl, add the pecans along with 1 tablespoon (15 ml) of the olive oil. Turn to coat them evenly and sprinkle lightly with ½ tablespoon of Cajun seasoning. Place on the other prepared baking sheet and roast in the oven until crunchy, about 10 minutes. Keep warm until serving.

4. Wash the carrot and with a vegetable peeler, slice a long peel off one side and discard. Hold the carrot tightly with one hand and, using the peeler, slice long lengthwise ribbons of carrot. Continue until the carrot is completely sliced. Toss the ribbons with a bit of olive oil and sprinkle lightly with ½ tablespoon of Cajun seasoning.

5. In a skillet over medium-high heat, add 2 tablespoons (30 ml) of the olive oil. Sprinkle the shrimp with ½ tablespoon of Cajun seasoning, add to the hot skillet, and sauté just until the shrimp turn pink and are done, about 5 minutes. Remove and keep warm until later.

6. In the same skillet, add 2 tablespoons (30 ml) more olive oil along with the onion, bell peppers, and celery. Cook until the peppers begin to brown, about 5 minutes, and then add the rice, green onion tops, and shredded carrot. Continue stirring to combine and warm through, about 5 minutes. Turn off the heat and keep warm.

recipe continues

7. In the bottom of two oversized bowls, layer half the shredded lettuce. Add a mound of the rice mixture to one side. Position 4 shrimp next to the rice, and mound the carrot ribbons and sweet potatoes alongside. Garnish with sprigs of fresh parsley and lay the pecans on top. Drizzle all the ingredients lightly with olive oil and 1 tablespoon (15 ml) each of fresh lemon juice. Sprinkle salt and coarse black pepper over the dish. Serve immediately.

NOTES I like building on top of the shredded lettuce; it wilts under the warmth of the ingredients, and the olive oil and lemon soak down to dress it. Feel free to omit the shrimp if you want a more vegetarian version. Think of the options you can include: perhaps red beans or lentils, kale or spinach, ground pork or cubed chicken.

BROWN RICE: A HEALTHIER ALTERNATIVE

Brown rice isn't my thing, but my daughter Lo teamed up with Roxanne to add a healthier regimen to my recipe repertoire. Like many dyed-in-the-wool Louisiana men, I am downright committed to white rice as a staple of my diet, and at this point in my life, I am hard pressed to change. That said, when I ran across a bag of brown rice on the supermarket shelf from my favorite rice brand, Supreme Rice, I stopped dead in my tracks.

With a bit of research, I found out that brown rice is the same grain as white rice. Pure and simple, when only the outer husk of a grain of rice is removed, the result is brown rice. You must remove the next two layers underneath the husk to produce white rice. So, it's those remaining side hulls and brans that are rich in proteins, thiamine, calcium, magnesium, fiber, and potassium. And for those (like me) that are trying to lose weight, brown rice is a healthful alternative given its low glycemic rating, which reduces insulin spikes. And in my Cajun Rice Bowl recipe, it tastes good, too.

BLACKENED CATFISH WITH LEMON ROSEMARY SAUCE

With the deep, dark flavor of pungent spices that seal in the moist flesh of wild-caught catfish, this dish is cloaked in a rich, lemony butter sauce that zings with taste. I love it so. Note that you MUST cook this dish outdoors on a gas grill or outdoor burner.

BLACKENING SPICE

3 tablespoons (24 g) smoked paprika

1 teaspoon cayenne pepper

1 teaspoon white pepper

1 teaspoon lemon pepper

1 teaspoon garlic powder

1 teaspoon onion powder

1 teaspoon dried rosemary

1 teaspoon dried thyme

1 teaspoon dried oregano

1 teaspoon salt

1 teaspoon ground black pepper

CATFISH

4 large (6 to 8 ounces [168 to 227 g] each) catfish fillets

½ cup (120 ml) melted unsalted butter

½ cup (120 g) unsalted butter, cut into 1-tablespoon (15 g) pats, divided

½ cup (120 ml) dry white wine

¼ cup (60 ml) freshly squeezed lemon juice

2 tablespoons (6 g) chopped fresh rosemary

4 sprigs fresh rosemary

8 lemon slices

BLACKENING SPICE

1. Add all of the ingredients to a food processor and blend. Pour into an airtight container and store at room temperature for up to 6 months.

CATFISH

1. On an outdoor gas grill or propane (or butane) burner, preheat a seasoned cast-iron skillet until very hot (this will take about 10 minutes).

2. Brush both sides of the fillets with the melted butter and coat with the blackening seasoning.

3. Add 2 pats of butter to the skillet and let melt. Using a large spatula, add a catfish fillet to the hot skillet and let cook on the first side for 1 minute (or a bit longer if your fillet is thicker) without moving. Gently turn the fish over and cook on the other side until done, about 1 minute, and remove to a platter to keep warm. Wipe the skillet clean and repeat with the remaining butter and fillets until all the fish is cooked.

4. Lower the heat under the skillet and add the wine, lemon juice, rosemary, and lemon slices. Bring to a simmer and reduce the wine by half, about 5 minutes.

5. To serve, add a blackened catfish fillet to a plate and spoon over the sauce along with 2 of the lemon slices. Garnish with a rosemary sprig.

THE BLACKENED BLUES

I love to season and blacken fish. But how I learned this technique is a story in itself, and one that I hope saves you the embarrassment that still haunts me. Although it was almost two decades ago, I remember it like it was yesterday, and I still say, "It's all your fault, Paul Prudhomme!"

Yes, it's your fault, Chef Paul, for being the Creole-cooking genius that inspired me to follow your steps into the dark, uncharted waters of the blackened abyss. Oh, I miss you so. I still idolize you; I still follow your recipes, and I will always devour your every word—your every delicious dish. But I will never blacken a fish again—indoors.

Admittedly, I've had my share of kitchen disasters that I chalk up to "just another learning experience." Like, never put half-frozen French fries into hot grease—duh! Never boil pasta in an unwatched pot—yuck! And never shave truffles with a razor-sharp mandoline—ouch! But nothing prepared me for the ultimate failure that still haunts me to this day.

Oh, you see it coming, don't you? Here's the culinary equation: screaming-hot cast-iron skillet + buttered fish fillets + monitored smoke alarm = Hello, fire department! Yep, this was one dinner party that went up in smoke and quickly moved outdoors—which is where it should have been in the first place.

The chef warned me. It was right there on his website, in the headnotes of the simple recipe: *If you don't have a commercial hood vent over your stove, this dish will set off every smoke alarm in your neighborhood! It's better to cook it outdoors on a gas grill or a butane burner.*

But who reads headnotes? Certainly not an experienced epicurean like me. Yeah, right! There are reasons that recipes are written with detailed, step-by-step instructions. Any good recipe writer (or follower) should know that. And to Chef Paul's credit, he knew it, too.

SMOTHERED PORK CHOPS WITH MUSHROOM GRAVY

Slow-simmered meat in a dark gravy spiked with the earthy flavor of mushrooms is just about as satisfying as food can get. I love how the meaty flavors of the pork release into the stock to form a rich sauce, and with the added roux, it slowly thickens. This stew pot is the crowning glory worthy of a steaming mound of long-grain white rice. Ah, the comforts of home in a black iron pot.

1 tablespoon (15 ml) bacon grease

1 cup (160 g) diced yellow onion

½ cup (75 g) diced red bell pepper

½ cup (75 g) diced green bell pepper

1 cup (120 g) diced celery

2 tablespoons (6 g) chopped flat-leaf parsley

2 cups (150 g) chopped mushrooms (button or baby portobellos)

4 (8-ounce [227 g]) bone-in pork sirloin chops

1 tablespoon (15 ml) Dark Cajun Roux (page 230)

4 cups (960 ml) chicken stock or water, plus more if needed

Kosher salt and freshly ground black pepper

2 teaspoons Cajun Seasoning Blend (page 231)

6 cups (1.2 kg) cooked long-grain white rice

Hot sauce, for serving

1. In a cast-iron pot over medium-high heat, add the bacon grease. Once sizzling, add the onion, bell peppers, celery, parsley, and mushrooms. Cook until the mushrooms begin to brown, about 8 minutes. Remove the vegetables to a platter and keep warm.

2. In the same pot, add the pork chops and brown on one side, turn, and brown on the other, about 10 minutes. Add the vegetables back to the pot along with the roux. Add the stock and season with salt, pepper, and the Cajun seasoning. Cover, lower the heat to a simmer, and cook for 1 hour 30 minutes or until the pork is tender and reaches an internal temperature of 145°F. Check every half hour to make sure there is still plenty of cooking liquid.

3. Serve the pork chops over a mound of white rice with hot sauce on the side.

SERVES 4

PREP TIME: 45 MINUTES
COOK TIME: 30 MINUTES
TOTAL TIME: 1 HOUR 15 MINUTES

BAKED FLOUNDER WITH SPRING ONION GRATIN

As the heady scent of anise releases from the fresh tarragon leaves and perfumes the cheesy cream reduction, this spring onion gratin crusts over and forms the perfect platform for saucing the freshly filleted flounder.

8 whole spring onions (bulbs and green tops attached)

1 pint (480 ml) heavy whipping cream

2 tablespoons (6 g) chopped fresh tarragon

½ teaspoon ground white pepper

½ cup (50 g) grated Parmesan cheese

4 (6-ounce [170 g]) flounder fillets

1 teaspoon Cajun Seasoning Blend (page 231)

Kosher salt and freshly ground black pepper

2 tablespoons (30 g) unsalted butter

1 teaspoon minced garlic

1 teaspoon freshly squeezed lemon juice

4 lemon slices, for garnish

1 tablespoon (6 g) grated lemon zest, for garnish

1 tablespoon (6 g) diced green onion tops, for garnish

1. Preheat the oven to 350°F (180°C).

2. Coat a 9 x 12-inch (23 x 30 cm) ovenproof baking dish with nonstick spray and add the spring onions in a row along the bottom. Pour in the cream and add the tarragon and white pepper. Place in the oven and bake until the cream begins to reduce and thicken by half, about 20 minutes. Remove from the oven and sprinkle with the Parmesan cheese. Return the dish to the oven and adjust the temperature to broil. Watch as the sauce thickens and the cheese begins to brown along the top and edges, about 1 minute. Turn off the oven and remove the dish before the cheese burns.

3. Sprinkle the flounder fillets with the Cajun seasoning and a pinch of salt and pepper.

4. In a skillet over medium-high heat, add the butter, garlic, and lemon juice, and once it begins sizzling, add the fillets. Cook on one side until browned, about 3 minutes, and then turn and cook on the other side for 2 minutes longer, or until the fish is cooked through. Remove from the pan and place the fillets into the baking dish on top of the spring onions and garnish with the lemon slices, lemon zest, and green onion. Place back into the warm oven for a couple of minutes and serve once your guests are seated.

JACKED-UP SHORT RIBS

So, here's the long and short of it: I am short rib obsessed. And with this recipe, I've done a Southern take on short ribs with a whiskey-infused sauce, a spicy addition of Cajun seasonings, and green chile tomatoes. With the addition of Jack Daniels whiskey, the resulting sauce has a smoky, oak barrel roundness that works perfectly with the beef. The tomato undertone turns this sauce an earthy brick red with an acidic bite that delivers a Louisiana Creole punch. Find well-marbled short ribs and don't worry about the fat content—fat adds flavor. I suggest using the thick, vertically cut, bone-in short ribs versus the thinner Asian-style ones.

8 meaty beef short ribs (see headnote)

½ cup (60 g) Cajun Seasoning Blend (page 231)

2 cups (240 g) all-purpose flour

¼ cup (60 ml) vegetable oil

1 cup (160 g) diced yellow onion

1 cup (120 g) diced celery

1 cup (150 g) diced green bell pepper

1 carrot, diced

2 cups (150 g) sliced baby portobello mushrooms

2 cloves garlic, minced

1 cup (240 ml) Jack Daniel's whiskey or bourbon

1 tablespoon (12 g) sugar

1 (10-ounce [280 g]) can mild diced tomatoes and green chiles, drained

3 tablespoons (45 g) tomato paste

2 cups (480 ml) beef stock

2 sprigs fresh rosemary, stems removed and chopped

2 bay leaves

Kosher salt and freshly ground black pepper

2 tablespoons (16 g) cornstarch

2 tablespoons (30 ml) water

1 cup (100 g) diced green onion tops

1. Preheat the oven to 375°F (190°C).

2. Sprinkle the short ribs lightly with some of the Cajun seasoning, using enough to coat all sides. In a large mixing bowl, add the flour and stir in the remaining Cajun seasoning. Add the short ribs and turn to coat with the flour.

3. In a cast-iron pot with a heavy lid over high heat, add the vegetable oil. Once the oil is smoking, turn the heat to medium, add the short ribs, and sauté the meat on all sides. Once they are completely browned, about 8 minutes, move them to a platter and set aside.

4. Immediately add the onion, celery, bell pepper, carrot, and mushrooms to the pot and decrease the heat to low. Sauté them slowly until the onions just begin to brown, about 5 minutes, and then add the garlic. Stir constantly and make sure the garlic does not burn.

5. Keep sautéing for 2 minutes until the onions begin to caramelize, and then carefully add the whiskey to deglaze the pot. Scrape the bottom of the pot, but be careful because the alcohol might ignite—it will subside once burned off.

6. While the whiskey is cooking down, add the sugar, diced tomatoes and green chiles, tomato paste, beef stock, rosemary, bay leaves, and a pinch of salt and a grind of black pepper. Add the short ribs back to the pot.

7. Cover the pot and lower the heat to a simmer. Let it braise on the stovetop for 30 minutes and then place in the hot oven for 1 hour.

8. Remove the pot from the oven and uncover. Check to see that the short ribs are fork tender. If so, place them on a serving platter.

9. Remove the vegetables and bay leaves from the sauce, reserving the mushrooms. With a large spoon, skim any fat from the top of the remaining liquid. On the stovetop, cook down the remaining sauce for 5 to 8 minutes to achieve the desired gravy thickness. If needed to thicken, mix the cornstarch and water to make a slurry and add to the pot. Or adjust with more beef stock to thin it out.

10. Return the short ribs and the mushrooms to the sauce and move the cast-iron pot to the center of the table for family-style serving. Garnish with the green onions.

SHRIMP AND EGG STEW

With its rich shrimp flavor and hard-boiled eggs soaking up the dark juices, this is a post–Mardi Gras tradition—a Lenten dish called Shrimp and Egg Stew. This is not gumbo, but I will admit it is gumbo-esque. There is a big difference: this recipe has a stew-like thickness. The intensity of flavor comes from a variety of sources: I use shrimp stock made from the shells and heads of shrimp that I peel, dried shrimp, and an extra layer of dark Cajun roux. Make this recipe any time of the year and astound your friends and family with a culturally significant (and delicious) Louisiana roots recipe.

4 large eggs

1 pound (455 g) large (31/40 count) Gulf shrimp, peeled and deveined

1 tablespoon (15 ml) vegetable oil

1 cup (160 g) chopped yellow onion

½ cup (60 g) chopped celery

½ cup (75 g) chopped green bell pepper

1 tablespoon (8 g) minced garlic

½ cup (25 g) chopped flat-leaf parsley

1 cup (100 g) diced green onions, divided

2 quarts (1.8 L) shrimp stock or water

6 tablespoons (90 ml) Dark Cajun Roux (page 230)

1 (4-ounce [112 g]) bag dried shrimp (see Sources, page 232)

1 tablespoon (8 g) Cajun Seasoning Blend (page 231)

1 tablespoon (8 g) freshly ground black pepper

Dash of hot sauce

Kosher salt

4 cups (800 g) cooked long-grain white rice

1. In a large pot with a lid, add the eggs. Cover with water and place over high heat. Once the water begins boiling, turn off the heat and cover. Let sit for 12 minutes. Drain and rinse the eggs under cold water until cooled. Peel the eggs and reserve for later use.

2. Butterfly the shrimp by slicing vertically along the inside to open up the shrimp. Place them in a bowl topped with ice and refrigerate until ready to use.

3. In a large pot over medium-high heat, add the oil. Once hot, add the onion, celery, and bell pepper. Cook until the onions turn translucent, about 5 minutes. Add the garlic, parsley, and ½ cup (50 g) of the green onions and cook for another 3 minutes. Add the stock and the roux and bring to a boil. Lower the heat to a simmer and stir until the roux begins to dissolve. Add the dried shrimp along with the boiled eggs and season with the Cajun seasoning, black pepper, and a dash of hot sauce.

4. Continue cooking over low heat for another 30 minutes, and add more stock (or water) to thin it out if it becomes too thick. Taste the stew and add salt as necessary. Just before serving, add the shrimp and cook until done, about 8 minutes. Turn off the heat and let everything soak until ready to serve. Serve over white rice and have the remaining ½ cup (50 g) green onion tops on the table for garnish.

EGGS IN THE STEWPOT

Adeline Landry Gary Fontenot is my mother-in-law's nanny (godmother). She grew up in Estherwood, Louisiana, and moved to Jennings on West Division Street in the 1960s. My wife Roxanne recalls her childhood summers spent at Nanny's and walking down the street every day to Cormier's Grocery Store (now Boudin King) for a Cajun snack—a link of boudin and an ice-cold Coca-Cola.

Rural Cajun farms in Acadiana are inland from the Gulf, and back in those days, fresh shrimp was hard to come by. When you were fortunate enough to get a bag of fresh Vermilion Bay shrimp, the black pot came out immediately. Catholic Cajun families were mostly large (Adeline had five children), so to extend the protein in the pot, Adeline gathered eggs from her laying hens and boiled them up. Soaking boiled eggs in a black pot of roux-infused stock is a tradition in gumbos and stews that is seen sparingly these days, but I still see it done on plate-lunch counters as well as old-school Cajun home cooking.

SWEET TEA-BRINED CHICKEN

I have an extra-large black iron skillet just for dishes like this one. I love the cast-iron conduction that evenly distributes the heat throughout the chicken and caramelizes the vegetables and lemons to add more flavor. And this chicken is cooked uncovered so that the skin will brown for that extra crispy snap when you bite into it. This is sure to become one of your favorite recipes.

1 (4-pound [1.8 kg]) whole chicken, butterflied

1 quart (960 ml) sweet tea, plus more if needed

¼ cup (60 ml) lemon juice

1 tablespoon (18 g) kosher salt

2 tablespoons (16 g) coarsely ground black pepper

1 tablespoon (8 g) Cajun Seasoning Blend (page 231)

¼ cup (60 ml) olive oil

1 lemon, halved

2 yellow onions, halved

2 heads garlic

4 tabasco peppers

4 sprigs fresh rosemary, plus more for garnish

1 bunch fresh flat-leaf parsley, plus more for garnish

1. In a large container with a lid, add the chicken. Add the tea and lemon juice. Add more tea if needed to cover the chicken. Place the top on the container and refrigerate for 4 hours or overnight.

2. Preheat the oven to 450°F (230°C).

3. Remove the chicken from the brine and pat dry. Combine the salt, pepper, and Cajun seasoning in a small bowl. Rub both sides of the chicken with the olive oil and sprinkle over the spices, coating each side.

4. In a large cast-iron skillet or a metal baking tray, place the lemon, onions, and garlic cut-side down. Layer the peppers, rosemary, and parsley around the skillet. Add the chicken on top, breast-side up. Bake for 20 minutes.

5. Decrease the temperature to 350°F (180°C) and bake until the internal temperature of the chicken reaches 165°F (74°C), approximately 1 hour, and the juices run clear.

6. To crisp the skin, turn your oven to broil (or to its highest temperature) and return the chicken to the oven, watching carefully to prevent burning. Broil until the top begins to brown and the skin is crispy, 3 to 5 minutes.

7. Remove the skillet from the oven and let the chicken rest for 10 minutes. Garnish with more of the fresh rosemary and parsley, and squeeze the roasted garlic and lemons over the chicken.

NOTES Prep time does not include brining. Butterfly the chicken by removing the backbone with kitchen scissors or a sharp knife. Be sure to remove any organ meats packaged inside the chicken.

LEMON THYME CHICKEN BREAST WITH CAULIFLOWER MASH

Lighten up with this boneless, skinless breast of chicken. It's flavor filled, herb infused, and laced with a delicate lemon thyme cream reduction. It's baked, broiled, and sauced to perfection, and, when paired with a delicious cauliflower mash, this chicken is center-of-the-plate perfection.

CAULIFLOWER MASH

1 large head cauliflower, green stems removed

½ cup (120 g) unsalted butter, plus more for serving

¼ cup (60 ml) heavy whipping cream

½ teaspoon white pepper

Kosher salt

LEMON THYME CHICKEN BREAST

3 large lemons, 2 quartered and 1 sliced into rounds, divided

4 large boneless, skinless chicken breasts

2 tablespoons (30 ml) melted butter

Kosher salt and freshly ground black pepper

4 sprigs flat-leaf parsley, plus more for garnish

4 sprigs thyme, plus more for garnish

1 cup (240 ml) heavy whipping cream

CAULIFLOWER MASH

1. In a large pot with a heavy lid and fitted with a steam basket, place the head of cauliflower stem-side down and add water. Turn the heat to high and, once boiling, lower the heat to medium, cover, and steam until fully cooked, about 30 minutes. Drain all the water.

2. Mash the cauliflower in the pot with a potato masher or handheld electric mixer until smooth. Add the butter, cream, and white pepper. Season to taste with salt. Keep warm until serving.

LEMON THYME CHICKEN BREAST

1. Preheat the oven to 350°F (180°C). Line a baking dish with foil.

2. Squeeze 1 lemon wedge on both sides of each chicken breast and brush with the melted butter. Sprinkle with salt and pepper.

3. Place the parsley, thyme, and lemon slices in the prepared baking dish, place the chicken breasts on top, and bake, uncovered, until fully cooked to an internal temperature of 175°F (80°C), about 25 minutes.

4. In a saucepan over medium-high heat, add the drippings and the herbs from the pan along with the cream. Cook until the cream reduces and thickens enough to coat the back of a spoon, about 10 minutes. Remove any stems. Season to taste with salt and pepper. Keep warm until serving.

5. Turn the oven to broil.

6. Place the chicken breasts under the broiler until the tops brown (watch carefully to prevent burning).

7. To serve, place a scoop of cauliflower mash in each of four shallow bowls and top with a chicken breast. Spoon the sauce over the chicken and garnish with a fresh sprig of thyme, some parsley, and the remaining lemon wedges.

PORK NECK BONE FRICASSEE

Succulent morsels of pork clinging tenderly to the bone swim alongside smoked pork sausage in a bowl of dark roux–based gravy. I love how the meat stays on the bone yet renders down to porky tenderness. This is inspired farmhouse cooking that is a mystery to most folks who have never explored adventurous cuts of meat.

¼ cup (60 ml) vegetable oil

2 cups (320 g) diced yellow onion

2 cups (300 g) diced green bell pepper

2 cups (240 g) diced celery

2 tablespoons (16 g) minced garlic

½ cup (25 g) chopped flat-leaf parsley

3 pounds (1.4 kg) pork neck bone, cut into 2-inch (5 cm) pieces

1 pound (455 g) chopped andouille sausage (see Sources, page 232)

1 pound (455 g) smoked pork sausage

3 quarts (2.7 L) chicken stock, plus water if needed

1½ teaspoons cayenne

1 tablespoon (8 g) Cajun Seasoning Blend (page 231)

1 cup (240 ml) Dark Cajun Roux, plus more if needed (page 230)

Kosher salt and freshly ground black pepper

Dash of hot sauce

8 cups (1.6 kg) cooked long-grain white rice, for serving

1 cup (100 g) diced green onion tops

1. In a large cast-iron pot with a lid over medium-high heat, add the oil. Once sizzling hot, add the onion, bell pepper, and celery. Sauté until the onion turns translucent, about 5 minutes. Add the garlic and parsley and stir until combined. Add the pork neck and sauté just until the pork and the vegetables begin to brown, about 8 minutes. Add the sausages. Add enough chicken stock to the pot to cover all the meat and vegetables, and scrape the bottom to loosen the brown bits of flavor.

2. Season with the cayenne and Cajun seasoning and stir to combine. Add the roux and stir. Bring the pot to a boil and then lower the heat to a simmer. Cover the pot and let it cook for 2 hours.

3. Uncover the pot and skim the surface of any excess oil. Taste the stew and if you prefer it thinner, add more stock or water. If you prefer it thicker, add more roux. Add salt and pepper to taste. Cover the pot and simmer for 30 minutes longer.

4. Sample the finished dish and add a dash of hot sauce if you like it spicier. Ladle the stew into large bowls over a mound of rice and garnish with the diced green onion tops.

MAKE FRIENDS WITH A BUTCHER

There's no clearer path to culinary enlightenment than through a butcher who can help you discover flavor-filled cuts of meat you never knew existed, and pork neck bone is one of those. Pork neck bone is an inexpensive (no, downright cheap) cut that is full of close-to-the-bone flavor. I buy my neck bone from my favorite butcher Billy Billeaud at Billeaud's Meat and Grocery in Broussard, LA (see Sources, page 232). Oxtail, stuffed turkey wings, seasoned rabbit, calf brisket, and hog's head cheese are all ingredients that have become mainstays in my kitchen. So, seek out a butcher (he will become your best friend) that can deliver these cuts and more. I guarantee that your friends and family will want the name of that butcher, too.

CHERRY PIE

You've just got to smile at the thought of a bite of my sweet cherry pie balancing the flavors of fresh fruit accented with a spike of pomegranate liqueur all baked in a crisp, flaky piecrust. I prefer the Bing variety versus the Rainier cherries. Bings are darker (red/black) with a classic balance of sweet and tart. If done right, cherry pie should be a study in culinary contrast: sweet versus tart, smooth versus crunchy. This one reaches that perfect combination easily. Serve with a scoop of vanilla ice cream.

PIECRUST

1½ cups (180 g) all-purpose flour, plus more for dusting

¾ teaspoon salt

¾ cup (180 g) unsalted butter, cut into chunks

5 tablespoons (75 ml) ice-cold water

FILLING

4 cups (620 g) fresh Bing cherries, stemmed and pitted

½ cup (100 g) sugar

1 teaspoon lemon juice

1 tablespoon (15 ml) melted butter

¼ cup (60 ml) pomegranate liqueur (optional)

¼ cup (30 g) cornstarch

1 egg, beaten

1 tablespoon (15 ml) water

PIECRUST

1. In a large mixing bowl, add the flour and salt and whisk to combine. With a pastry cutter or tines of a fork, gradually cut in the cold butter and combine the mixture until it reaches the texture of coarse cornmeal.

2. Gradually add the cold water until it is incorporated and roll the dough together with your hands to form a ball.

3. Divide the ball into two smaller balls and cover each with a wet paper towel to keep them from drying out. Refrigerate until ready to use.

FILLING

1. Make sure the cherry stems and pits have all been removed and place the cherries in a large mixing bowl. Add the sugar, lemon juice, butter, and pomegranate liqueur (if using) and mix with a large spoon. Using the back of the spoon, mash some of the cherries to release their juice. Sprinkle the cornstarch evenly over the mixture and stir to combine. Let the mixture rest for 30 minutes at room temperature.

2. Preheat the oven to 425°F (220°C). Have ready a 9-inch (23 cm) aluminum pie pan.

3. On a clean countertop or a large cutting board sprinkled with flour, add one of the balls of dough. Flatten the dough ball down and begin rolling it out with a rolling pin dusted with flour. Roll into a 10-inch (25 cm) circle. Move the sheet of dough to the pie pan and let the excess dough hang over the sides. Pour the cherry mixture into the center and smooth out evenly.

4. Using the same procedure as the first, roll out the second piecrust to approximately 10 inches (25 cm). Gently add the second piecrust on top of the cherry filling and use your fingers to pinch the edges together until they seal into a fluted pattern. Trim off any excess dough. Use a sharp knife to cut a hole in the center to vent the steam.

5. In a small bowl, add the beaten egg and water. Whisk to combine and brush the top and edges of the piecrust with the egg wash.

6. Place the pie on a baking sheet, center it in the preheated oven, and bake for 15 minutes. Lower the heat to 350°F (180°C) and bake until the crust is golden brown, about another 45 minutes. (Note: Keep an eye on the browning and cover with aluminum foil if the crust is darkening too much.)

7. Remove from the oven and let cool for at least 30 minutes before slicing. The pie is best served at room temperature.

APRICOT PISTACHIO COBBLER

For me, cobbler is the official dessert of the South. And in this version, I combine a few eclectic ingredients that sing to me with a French harmony of flavors. Fresh apricots rock. At their vine-ripened peak, juices flow and the fleshy interior of these little orbs welcome you with just one bite full of flavor. Baked in a honey-kissed recipe with the crunch of pistachios, this is one easy dessert to cobble together. Serve with whipped cream or a scoop of vanilla bean ice cream.

2 tablespoons (30 ml) coconut oil, butter, or vegetable oil

12 fresh ripe apricots, halved, stemmed and seeded

1½ cups (180 g) all-purpose flour

½ cup (100 g) sugar

1 tablespoon (8 g) baking powder

1 tablespoon (8 g) cornstarch

1 teaspoon ground cinnamon

½ teaspoon salt

1 egg, beaten

½ cup (170 g) honey

1 teaspoon vanilla extract

4 tablespoons (60 g) melted unsalted butter

½ cup (60 g) plus 1 tablespoon (9 g) shelled pistachios, divided

1. Preheat the oven to 375°F (190°C).

2. Grease an ovenproof baking dish with the coconut oil and scatter the apricots in the bottom.

3. In a mixing bowl, add the flour, sugar, baking powder, cornstarch, cinnamon, and salt. Mix thoroughly, eliminating any lumps.

4. In another mixing bowl, add the egg, honey, vanilla, and butter. Whisk to combine.

5. Add the dry ingredients to the wet and combine thoroughly until it resembles wet sand. Add ½ cup (60 g) of the pistachios and mix to combine. Pour over the apricots. Sprinkle the remaining 1 tablespoon (9 g) pistachios evenly over the mixture. Place in the oven and bake until golden brown, 45 to 60 minutes. Serve hot.

GRAPEFRUIT BASIL COCKTAIL

Slipping into warmer weather with a refreshing cocktail is the best way I know how to cool off in south Louisiana. And when fresh grapefruits hit the produce stands and markets, I break out my juicer and best bottle of gin. Garnished with a bouquet of fresh basil from my herb garden, the fragrant scent mingles on the nose with each satisfying sip. Yes, I'll have another, please.

6 ounces (180 ml) freshly squeezed grapefruit juice, strained

1 jigger (1.5 ounces [45 ml]) gin, silver rum, or vodka

1 jigger (1.5 ounces [45 ml]) citrus liqueur, such as triple sec

½ jigger (0.75 ounce [23 ml]) cherry juice

½ jigger (0.75 ounce [23 ml]) simple syrup (optional)

Club soda

1 sprig fresh basil, for garnish

3 Bing cherries, for garnish

1 grapefruit slice, for garnish

1. Fill a shaker (with a tight-fitting lid) halfway with ice. Add the grapefruit juice, gin, citrus liqueur, cherry juice, and simple syrup. Shake well and strain into a 12-ounce (360 ml) glass filled with ice cubes. Top with club soda and stir. Garnish with fresh basil, cherries, and a grapefruit slice.

CHAPTER 2
SUMMER

SUMMERS IN LOUISIANA ARE SPECIAL. Fresh produce and coastal seafood flood the roadside stands, farmers' markets, and rural groceries. There is an endless variety of fruits and vegetables, along with fresh shrimp and crabs, that signal the season. I drive the byways in search of the best-quality ingredients I can find, and along the way, I discover new and enlightening recipes to use them in. It reminds me of a summer trip Roxanne and I once made that led me to write this book.

The summer I spent years ago traveling the back roads of southern France was a culinary epiphany of sorts as I connected to the food of the region. I am a student of French cooking, and while I'm not classically trained, I've had a lifelong curiosity for French culinary history and technique. I find that French people elevate cooking to an art form; they approach it all quite seriously. For me, it is both fascinating and romantic.

That summer, my wife and I fell in love with the terroir and the locals that inhabit the villages, farms, markets, and shops of Provence. Author Peter Mayle was partially responsible for my itinerary; I was reading his best-selling novel *A Year in Provence* and retraced his steps through the region. Aix-en-Provence was our home base where we ventured out for day trips in search of cultural adventure. At every turn, every fork in the road, there were exciting discoveries. That trip was the catalyst for my love affair with the cooking of Louisiana.

Although a vast ocean of differences separates the two regions, they have so much in common: a cultural reverence for food, traditions, and customs tied to French heritage, and a colorful cast of characters who make up the local foodways. Farm-to-table sourcing at local markets has upped the culinary game here in Louisiana, and the expanding list of growers and processors has elevated the quality of my home region's food culture.

For me, two dishes define the provincial cooking of southern France, and they both list garlic as a potent ingredient that shows up in many Louisiana recipes. One is a rustic chicken with forty cloves of garlic, a Provençal main course. The other is ratatouille, a classic side dish that shows up often on the center of the French farmhouse table with a baguette of bread and a jug of red wine. It's a simple vegetable dish—some might say a peasant dish—but I believe it represents the philosophy of French cooking and easily connects to my Louisiana roots in my version of Farm-to-Table Ratatouille.

SERVES 6

PREP TIME: 45 MINUTES
COOK TIME: 30 MINUTES
TOTAL TIME: 1 HOUR 15 MINUTES

FARM-TO-TABLE RATATOUILLE

Crisp farm-to-table vegetables, vine-ripened Creole tomatoes, and homegrown herbs are sautéed and stewed down in my ratatouille, the Louisiana version of a classic French Provençal side dish. Follow my lead and improvise in making this classic vegetable side dish with the freshest ingredients you can find.

¼ cup (60 ml) olive oil

3 medium yellow onions, roughly chopped

2 cups (165 g) roughly chopped eggplant

2 cups (240 g) roughly chopped mirliton squash, zucchini, or yellow squash

3 sweet peppers or bell peppers, cut into chunks

2 tablespoons (16 g) minced garlic

1 cup (50 g) roughly chopped flat-leaf parsley, plus more for garnish

2 large tomatoes, quartered

2 tablespoons (30 g) tomato paste

¼ cup (60 ml) chicken stock

1 tablespoon (3 g) chopped fresh rosemary

1 teaspoon dried oregano

½ teaspoon dried thyme

Kosher salt and freshly ground black pepper

6 medium-size okra pods

Extra-virgin olive oil, for finishing

1. In a large skillet with a heavy lid over medium-high heat, add the oil. Once hot, add the onions. On top of the onions, add the eggplant, squash, peppers, garlic, and parsley. Once the onions begin to brown, about 5 minutes, stir the mixture by scraping from the bottom with a spatula and incorporate all of the vegetables.

2. Lower the heat to medium and add the tomatoes, tomato paste, and chicken stock and stir to combine. Add the rosemary, oregano, and thyme, and season with salt and pepper.

3. Stir the mixture and add the okra pods on top. Cover the skillet, lower the heat, and let simmer for 15 minutes until the vegetables are cooked through but not breaking down. Don't stir the okra, or they will release their sticky mucus; just let them steam on top. Turn off the heat and let rest before serving.

4. To serve family style, place the skillet of ratatouille on the table, drizzle with olive oil, and garnish with a sprig of parsley.

TOP TOMATOES

The stack of locally grown Creole tomatoes I discovered at my local produce market spoke to me in a culinary love language that only I can decipher. They whispered sweetness.

But how do you select a top tomato? The key is threefold: Visually inspect the tomato for brightness and a blemish-free appearance. Even one little black spot or small bruise is a signal of the spoilage that might be hiding inside. Gently caress the fruit, and if your touch is met with a mushy feel, keep walking. But if you feel a dense, heavy ripeness, it usually means the tomato is full of juice and ready for eating. And finally, bring it to your nose and smell for a fresh, earthy scent; it should be a slight, pleasing aroma of sweetness. And do not ever buy tomatoes of any kind pre-packaged and wrapped tightly in plastic. My motto: If you can't inspect them, reject them.

BOUDIN QUICHE

Oh, I love it so. Rich, farm-fresh eggs from a local family farm's henhouse gently encase spicy Cajun boudin spiked with a medley of aromatic vegetables, all neatly baked in a crumbly piecrust. This easy recipe is the perfect breakfast, lunch, or dinner dish; it's as good hot out of the oven as it is reheated a day later.

1 (9-inch [23 cm]) piecrust, homemade (page 66) or store-bought

1 pound (455 g) Cajun boudin, homemade (page 229) or store-bought (see Sources, page 232)

½ cup (80 g) diced yellow onion

2 tablespoons (18 g) diced green bell pepper

2 tablespoons (18 g) diced red bell pepper

2 tablespoons (16 g) diced celery

2 tablespoons (6 g) chopped flat-leaf parsley, plus sprigs for garnish

1 teaspoon Cajun Seasoning Blend (page 231)

8 eggs, beaten

2 strips smoked bacon, cooked until crispy

1. Preheat the oven to 350°F (180°C).

2. If the piecrust is not already in a pie pan, place it in one, and pinch the edges.

3. If the boudin is in links, remove the meat from the casing and distribute it evenly around the piecrust.

4. Distribute the diced onion, bell peppers, celery, and parsley evenly throughout the piecrust.

5. Sprinkle lightly with the Cajun Seasoning and pour over enough of the eggs to cover all the ingredients.

6. Crumble the bacon and spread it evenly over the top.

7. Place the pie in the hot oven and bake until the egg mixture sets and the crust is brown, 45 minutes to 1 hour.

8. Slice into portions and garnish with a sprig of parsley.

CREOLE CIOPPINO

Louisiana Creole tomatoes, the Cajun holy trinity (onions, celery, and bell pepper) of vegetables, crusty French bread, and fresh Gulf shrimp, oysters, blue crab, and snapper are the building blocks of a righteous bowl of cioppino. My fish soup recipe is as simple as it sounds, but just like its Pacific Coast counterpart, it depends on freshness. Wherever you live, you must find a fishmonger you can trust to source the quality ingredients necessary for a truly memorable bowl of cioppino.

2 tablespoons (30 ml) olive oil

4 boneless fillets Gulf snapper or other firm white fish

Kosher salt and freshly ground black pepper

2 cups (320 g) chopped yellow onion

1 cup (120 g) diced celery

1 cup (150 g) diced green bell pepper

½ cup (150 g) chopped yellow bell pepper

½ cup (75 g) chopped red bell pepper

½ cup (75 g) chopped tasso or smoked ham

1 tablespoon (8 g) minced garlic

4 anchovy fillets, chopped

1 tablespoon (3 g) fresh thyme leaves

1 teaspoon dried oregano

½ cup (25 g) chopped flat-leaf parsley

1 teaspoon red pepper flakes

1 tablespoon (12 g) jarred dry light roux or all-purpose flour

1 cup (240 ml) dry white wine

2 cups (360 g) chopped ripe tomatoes, preferably Louisiana Creole tomatoes

1 (15-ounce [420 g]) can tomato sauce

1 (8-ounce [227 ml]) bottle clam juice

3 cups (720 ml) seafood stock

2 Louisiana blue crabs, cleaned and cut in half

2 bay leaves

8 oysters, in the shell

16 colossal (8/10 count) shrimp, peeled, tail on, and deveined

1 pound (455 g) white lump crabmeat, picked over for shells and cartilage

1 cup (140 g) crawfish tail meat (see Sources, page 232)

4 slices French bread, grilled, for serving

½ cup (50 g) diced green onion tops

1. In a cast-iron pot with a heavy lid over medium-high heat, add the olive oil. Sprinkle the fish fillets lightly with salt and pepper, and add to the pot. Cook for 2 minutes on the first side. Turn the fish over and cook on the other side until just done, 1 to 2 minutes depending on the thickness of your fillets. With a spatula, carefully remove the fish to a platter and keep warm for later.

2. In the same pot, add the onion, celery, bell peppers, and tasso and sauté until the onion turns translucent, about 5 minutes. Add the garlic, anchovies, thyme, oregano, parsley, and red pepper flakes and sauté for 3 minutes.

3. Sprinkle the dry roux over the vegetables in the pot and stir to incorporate. Add the wine to deglaze the pot (be careful of flames), and cook off the alcohol, about 5 minutes. Add the tomatoes, tomato sauce, clam juice, and seafood stock. Stir to combine and then add the crab and bay leaves. Bring to a boil and lower the heat to a simmer. Cover and cook for 30 minutes. Taste the soup and adjust the seasoning with salt and pepper. Turn off the heat until ready to serve. Remove the bay leaves.

4. With a towel and an oyster knife, pry open the oysters, reserving any oyster liquor inside. Discard the top shell and drain any liquor into the pot. Reserve the bottom half shell oyster, but do not loosen the meat from the shell. Keep cold until ready to serve.

5. When ready to serve, reheat the pot to a simmer, add the shrimp, and cook for 3 minutes. Add the oyster half shells, crabmeat, and crawfish to the pot. Lightly stir to incorporate the seafood into the simmering liquid. Cook for 1 minute and serve immediately.

6. To serve, place a grilled French bread slice in the bottom of a large individual bowl. Add a fillet of sautéed fish to each bowl. Spoon the simmering soup over, being careful to distribute the seafood evenly among your guests. Garnish with a sprinkle of green onion.

BAKED EGGS IN TASSO CREAM

Oven-baked eggs oozing their liquid sunshine and swimming in a sea of smoked tasso-infused cream is a thing of beauty—and taste. I've made this easy breakfast dish for years, and it still astounds me how flavorful and straightforward it is. With a slice of toasted French bread for sopping up the yolk, it is filling as well.

2 tablespoons (30 g) unsalted butter

½ cup (80 g) finely chopped yellow onion

1 cup (140 g) chopped tasso (see Sources, page 232) or smoked ham

2 cups (480 ml) heavy cream

1 cup (60 g) fresh basil leaves, stemmed, plus more for garnish

1 teaspoon Cajun Seasoning Blend (page 231)

8 large eggs

Kosher salt and freshly ground black pepper

½ cup (50 g) diced green onion tops

Toasted French bread slices, for serving

1. Preheat the oven to 350°F (180°C). Line a baking sheet with foil. Have ready four small, shallow ovenproof baking dishes (or ramekins).

2. In a wide, 10-inch (25 cm) skillet over medium-high heat, add the butter, onion, and tasso. Sauté until the onion turns translucent and the tasso begins to brown, 5 to 8 minutes. Add the cream and continue stirring as the cream simmers and begins to reduce. Add the basil. Large bubbles will appear in the cream as the moisture releases and it thickens. Once it reduces to a sauce-like consistency and the basil leaves are wilted, about 5 minutes, lower the heat to a simmer.

3. Add the Cajun seasoning, stir, and remove the skillet from the heat.

4. Gently (being careful not to break the yolks) add 2 eggs to each of the baking dishes. Divide the sauce evenly among the dishes. Place the baking dishes on the prepared baking sheet and bake on the upper rack of the hot oven. Watch carefully (you may need to rotate the baking sheet) and bake only until the whites set with a still sunny-side-up runny yolk, about 10 minutes.

5. Season with a pinch of kosher salt and a half-grind of black pepper. Top with a sprinkle of diced green onion. Garnish with a sprig of basil, and serve with toasted French bread slices.

PREP TIME: 30 MINUTES
COOK TIME: 35 MINUTES
TOTAL TIME: 1 HOUR 5 MINUTES

GULF COAST SHRIMP BOIL

I love shrimp season in Louisiana. The opening of the Vermilion Bay inshore waters in late May signals the start of an endless summer supply of fresh Gulf shrimp. While I'm ready with a stack of recipes, there is no denying that a simple backyard shrimp boil is the purest (and best) recipe for shrimp from Louisiana waters. And while it's easy, there is one cardinal rule for a shrimp boil: Do Not Overcook. What you do from there can only elevate the experience. Other ingredients? Beer? Spice level? Dipping sauce? Did I say the beer? Let's get to boiling.

3 gallons (11.5 L) water

1 cup (288 g) salt

3 (3-ounce [85 g]) bags shrimp boil seasoning (see Sources, page 232) or 1 cup (120 g) Cajun Seasoning Blend (page 231)

4 lemons, halved

3 pounds (1.4 kg) small red potatoes

12 ears frozen corn on the cob

5 pounds (2.2 kg) smoked pork sausage links, cut into portions

6 pounds (2.7 kg) large head-on fresh Gulf shrimp

½ cup (60 g) Cajun Seasoning Blend (optional, page 231)

Cocktail sauce, for serving

1. In a large stockpot over high heat, bring the water to a rolling boil. Add the salt, bags of shrimp boil seasoning, and lemon halves. Continue to boil for 5 minutes as the water seasons.

2. Add the potatoes and let boil for 10 minutes. Add the corn and sausage and boil for another 10 minutes. Add the shrimp and boil for 2 minutes longer, and then turn off the heat. Let the shrimp and all the other ingredients sit in the water for 5 minutes and then remove.

3. Pile the shrimp, potatoes, corn, and sausage together on a newspaper-lined table. Sprinkle on the Cajun seasoning if desired. Serve with cocktail sauce or your favorite dipping sauce and ice-cold beer.

NOTES Plan on at least 1 pound (455 g) of shrimp per person. I add corn, potatoes, and smoked sausage, but you can boil whatever you like alongside your shrimp.

TOMATO CHEESE TART

One bite of flaky piecrust infused with herbs and cheeses and topped with ripe tomatoes will send your taste buds to that delicious culinary hiding place in your brain. You know where I mean, and you know that you don't visit that place as often as you'd like or need or crave. Once you learn the art of the tart in this recipe, you've got the master key. Serve this beauty with a side salad and a glass of wine.

1 (9-inch [23 cm]) store-bought refrigerated rolled piecrust dough

All-purpose flour, for dusting

1 large ripe in-season red tomato

1 large ripe in-season yellow tomato

Sea salt

2 tablespoons (30 g) ricotta cheese

2 tablespoons (12 g) grated Romano cheese

½ cup (60 g) grated Gouda cheese

1 tablespoon (6 g) grated lemon zest

1 teaspoon freshly squeezed lemon juice

¼ cup (25 g) diced green onion tops

½ cup (15 g) baby arugula

1 teaspoon minced garlic

1 large egg

Freshly ground black pepper

½ cup (80 g) thinly sliced red onion

3 green onions, steamed in the microwave and drained

½ cup (70 g) red and yellow cherry tomatoes, sliced

½ cup (30 g) fresh basil leaves

1. Preheat the oven to 375°F (190°C). Coat a 9-inch (23 cm) fluted tart pan with removable bottom with nonstick spray.

2. Remove the piecrust from the refrigerator and let it come to room temperature. Carefully remove the piecrust from the package and onto a work surface dusted with flour. Sprinkle the top with flour and begin rolling out the dough into a larger circle. Using a tape measure, roll it into 10½-inch (26.7 cm) round. This diameter will give you enough excess to build the edges along the rim of the tart pan.

3. Place the piecrust in the prepared pan and press it into the fluted edges. Remove any excess dough to form a clean edge. If you have any gaps in the piecrust, repair it by using excess dough pressed into the crust with your warm hands. Using a fork, prick the piecrust all over the bottom and the sides. Line the crust with foil and fill with pie weights (or dried beans or raw rice). Bake in the oven until brown around the edges, about 25 minutes. (It's important to prebake the piecrust until crispy or the filling will make it soggy.) Remove from the oven and remove the foil and pie weights.

4. Slice the tomatoes into ¼-inch (6 mm)-thick rounds and place on a paper towel–lined tray. Sprinkle with salt and place another sheet of paper towel on top. Place a tray or cutting board on top to add weight and draw out the excess moisture in the tomatoes.

5. In a large mixing bowl, add the ricotta, Romano, and Gouda cheeses and stir to combine. Add the lemon zest, lemon juice, green onion, arugula, garlic, and egg. Stir the egg into the mixture and combine. Season with salt and coarsely ground black pepper.

6. Pour the filling into the piecrust, making sure to spread it evenly to the edges. Lay the sliced red onions over the filling and press down. Place the tomato slices on top, arranging them in alternating colors. Arrange the green onions on top and fill in the gaps with the cherry tomatoes. Sprinkle with salt and pepper.

7. Cut 2-inch (5 cm)-wide strips of aluminum foil to line the edges of the piecrust to prevent overcooking. Lower the oven temperature to 350°F (180°C) and bake the tart until the filling sets and the edges of the pastry begin to brown, 30 to 40 minutes. Remove from the oven and let cool for 30 minutes. Pop the bottom of the tart pan from the fluted metal ring by placing it over a can of vegetables. Slide the tart off the bottom and onto a cake stand or platter and slice. Grind black pepper over the top and sprinkle with the fresh basil leaves. Serve at room temperature.

NOTES If using frozen pie dough, allow 2 hours to defrost. It is essential to source ripe, seasonal tomatoes. Heirlooms arrive early in the spring, and look for hothouse tomatoes or the Creole variety of Louisiana tomatoes in summer. I used cheeses that I had on hand; feel free to try this with Gruyere, Parmesan, or even goat cheese.

SERVES 4

PREP TIME: 45 MINUTES
COOK TIME: 5 MINUTES
TOTAL TIME: 50 MINUTES

RADISH AND GOAT CHEESE TARTINE

So, what exactly is a tartine? By definition, it's a French open-faced sandwich with sweet or savory ingredients. And this tartine is locally sourced and built on a platform of farm-to-table flavor featuring watermelon radishes. Crisp and flavor filled, this radish hybrid has a spicy profile that punches these tartines with a peppery finish. And my creamy goat cheese brings a mellow sweetness and a textural smoothness to underscore these crisp vegetables. It's a Saturday morning farmers' market recipe; just use whatever is fresh and seasonal.

4 slices whole-grain bread

¼ cup (60 ml) extra-virgin olive oil, divided

¼ cup (35 g) goat cheese

1 cup (30 g) mixed lettuce leaves

3 large watermelon radishes or regular radishes, sliced into thin rounds

2 tablespoons (6 g) alfalfa sprouts

Sea salt

1. Preheat the oven to 350°F (180°C).

2. Using a round cookie cutter (I use the top to my cocktail shaker), cut out a circle from each slice of bread and discard the crust. Lightly brush the circle with some of the olive oil and place on a baking sheet. Place in the oven and toast until the bread just begins to brown, about 5 minutes (watch carefully). Remove to a cutting board.

3. Spread the bread rounds with the goat cheese, add lettuce leaves, and place 3 radish slices on top. Sprinkle with the sprouts and drizzle over the remaining olive oil. Sprinkle on some sea salt and serve immediately.

CRABMEAT SALAD

SERVES 4

PREP TIME: 45 MINUTES
TOTAL TIME: 45 MINUTES

Lumps of flaky white crabmeat picked from the shell of blue crabs are treated delicately with fresh aromatics, creamy avocado, crisp apple, and a smooth cloak of mayo. This light summertime crabmeat salad is a refreshing break from heartier Southern fare. A glass of chilled rosé wine would be delightful with this light dish.

1 pound (455 g) white lump crabmeat, such as Gulf blue crab

¼ cup (30 g) finely diced celery

¼ cup (35 g) finely diced green bell pepper

2 tablespoons (20 g) finely diced red onion

2 tablespoons (6 g) chopped flat-leaf parsley, plus more for garnish

2 tablespoons (6 g) chopped basil

1 tablespoon (15 g) mayonnaise

1 ripe but firm avocado, peeled, pitted, and cubed

1 apple, such as Red Delicious, peeled, cored, and finely diced

1 tablespoon (15 ml) freshly squeezed lemon juice

Kosher salt and freshly ground black pepper

Lemon slice, for garnish

1. Add the crabmeat to a bowl and carefully inspect it, removing any shells or cartilage. Cover and refrigerate to chill.

2. In a large mixing bowl, add the celery, bell pepper, onion, parsley, basil, and mayonnaise. Stir to combine and then add the avocado, apple, and crabmeat. Add the lemon juice and lightly sprinkle with salt and a quick grind of pepper. Very gingerly, combine the mixture, being careful not to break up the crabmeat. Cover with plastic wrap and refrigerate until ready to serve.

3. To serve, add the mixture to a chilled glass bowl and garnish with sprigs of parsley and fresh lemon slices. Serve on a platter with lettuce leaves and sliced tomatoes surrounding. Optionally, fill the halved avocado hulls with the crabmeat salad and garnish individually with a lemon slice.

CORN CASSEROLE

Using fresh-shucked corn cut off the cob, this casserole is a masterwork of balance in taste and texture. A hint of spice plays against the corn's sweetness, and the creamy cheese oozes texturally with the crunchy contrast of aromatic onion, bell pepper, and celery. But the real genius of this recipe is the lighter-than-air lift that eggs give it; it's an elegant soufflé-like richness that beckons you back for more.

12 ears fresh yellow corn, husks and silks removed

½ cup (120 g) butter

2 tablespoons (16 g) all-purpose flour

½ cup (80 g) diced yellow onion

½ cup (75 g) finely diced green bell pepper

½ cup (75 g) finely diced red bell pepper

½ cup (60 g) finely diced celery

¼ cup (12 g) chopped flat-leaf parsley

2 (12-ounce [360 ml]) cans evaporated milk

3 large eggs, beaten

1½ cups (180 g) shredded sharp Cheddar cheese

1 tablespoon (8 g) Cajun Seasoning Blend (page 231)

1 teaspoon white pepper

1 teaspoon sugar

1 teaspoon kosher salt

1 teaspoon freshly ground black pepper

1. Preheat the oven to 350°F (180°C). Coat a 9 x 13-inch (23 x 33 cm) ovenproof baking dish with nonstick spray.

2. With a sharp knife, cut the kernels of corn off the cobs, scraping as close to the cob as possible to get as much of the corn "milk" as you can.

3. In a heavy cast-iron skillet over medium-high heat, melt the butter. When the butter begins sizzling, add the flour and stir to make a light blond roux. Add the onion, bell peppers, celery, and parsley, and sauté for 2 minutes.

4. Add the evaporated milk and stir to thicken the mixture to a sauce-like consistency.

5. In a mixing bowl, add the beaten eggs and slowly begin whisking in the hot vegetable mixture. Once the egg is tempered, return it all back to the skillet. Add the corn along with the cheese. Add the Cajun seasoning, white pepper, sugar, salt, and black pepper and stir to combine.

6. Pour the corn mixture into the prepared baking dish and place in the oven. Bake until the top just begins to brown around the edges, about 1 hour. Serve immediately.

BACKYARD BEANS

Now that the summer season is in full swing, it's time to roll out the barbecue pits and light the grills for outdoor cooking. And a pot of baked beans is certain to be on the menu. These beans are laced with tender chunks of pickled pork, whose flavor bursts and mixes with the red beans sweetened with the familiar taste of Louisiana sugarcane molasses. All cooked down into a thickly glazed finish, this meaty bean pot brings a magical taste to your backyard cookout.

2 (1-pound [455 g]) packages dried red beans

1½ cups (240 g) chopped yellow onion

½ cup (60 g) diced celery

½ cup (75 g) diced green bell pepper

1 (1-pound [455 g]) package pickled pork (see Sources, page 232)

¾ cup (160 g) packed dark brown sugar

½ cup (170 g) sugarcane molasses, such as Steen's (see Sources, page 232)

1 tablespoon (10 g) chopped canned chipotle chiles, plus 1 tablespoon (15 ml) adobo sauce

1 tablespoon (11 g) Creole mustard or coarse-grained mustard

1 tablespoon (18 g) kosher salt

1 tablespoon (8 g) freshly ground black pepper

1 teaspoon cayenne pepper

2 bay leaves

4 cups (960 ml) water

1. Soak the beans by adding them to a covered container and filling with water. Cover and let soak overnight or for a minimum of 8 hours. Drain and set aside.

2. In a large slow cooker (I use an 8-quart [7.2 L] size), add the beans along with the onion, celery, and bell pepper and stir to combine. Add the pork, brown sugar, molasses, chiles with sauce, and mustard; stir to combine. Season with the salt, pepper, and cayenne, and add the bay leaves. Add the water and stir to combine. Cover and cook on high for 10 hours (or overnight) until the beans are tender.

3. Once the beans are tender, turn off the slow cooker and remove the bay leaves. Serve from the ceramic pot or pour the beans into a serving dish.

PICKLED MEAT

What many old-school Cajun and Creole cooks refer to as "pickle meat" has been around since the Civil War era. Before refrigeration, preserving slabs of pork in a salt/sugar curing brine was the only way to have a steady supply on hand. The tradition of adding pickled pork (also called salt pork) to a pot of slow-simmered beans, greens, or any vegetable dish that has a long cooking time is still practiced today by home cooks and restaurant chefs alike. Perfectly cured and precut into cubes, a slab of boneless pork adds bright flavor and spice to a pot of red beans. And the meat that cooks down in the pot is one of the highlights of my Backyard Beans dish.

TOMATO SANDWICH ON SOURDOUGH WITH GARLIC AIOLI

Fresh homegrown tomatoes bursting with flavor are the stars in this down-home sandwich. With the crisp snap of the first bite of grilled sourdough, you'll taste the combination of smooth goat cheese and creamy garlic aioli as the intense juice of ripe tomato flows over your tongue. Your taste receptors will be in overdrive as the flavors meld together into the perfect sandwich bite.

1 large loaf sourdough bread

Extra-virgin olive oil

Sea salt

4 large ripe heirloom, hothouse, or Creole tomatoes, in assorted colors

1 tablespoon (6 g) finely minced garlic

1 tablespoon (15 ml) freshly squeezed lemon juice

1 cup (240 g) quality mayonnaise

1 (8-ounce [227 g] package) goat cheese

2 cups (60 g) loosely packed baby arugula

Freshly ground black pepper

4 sprigs fresh basil leaves, for garnish

1. Prepare a grill to medium heat. Clean and oil the grates.

2. Slice the bread into thick slices and brush both sides with olive oil. Place on the grill grates. Watch carefully as the bread toasts on one side, and then turn and toast on the other. Sprinkle the bread slices with sea salt. Remove and keep warm.

3. Slice the tomatoes into thick rounds and place on paper towels. Sprinkle with sea salt and place another paper towel on top. Let sit for 30 minutes, as some of the moisture escapes and the tomato flavor concentrates.

4. Meanwhile, make the aioli by whisking together the garlic, lemon juice, and mayonnaise in a mixing bowl. Refrigerate the aioli until ready to use.

5. To assemble the sandwich, spread the top bread with goat cheese. Spread aioli on the bottom bread and arrange the arugula on top. Place the tomatoes over the greens and lightly drizzle with olive oil. Sprinkle with sea salt and coarsely ground black pepper. Garnish with a sprig of fresh basil and serve open face with the top bread to this side.

BACON-WRAPPED MEAT LOAF

I tinkered with this recipe until I found a combination that delivers on a meat loaf promise—moist meat, balanced taste, and delicious surprises. In the center of it all is a stuffing of spinach and pepper Jack cheese that oozes flavor and keeps the meat from drying out. And the icing on this loaf is a spectacular bacon weave glazed with a ketchup and red pepper jelly combination. It's a fun dinnertime project with dramatic results, but in the end, it's just meat loaf—comforting meat loaf. Mashed potatoes would be a traditional side dish for the perfect comfort meal.

1 tablespoon (15 ml) olive oil

1 cup (160 g) finely diced yellow onion

½ cup (60 g) finely diced celery

½ cup (75 g) finely diced green bell pepper

1 tablespoon (6 g) minced garlic

1 tablespoon (3 g) chopped rosemary

2 tablespoons (6 g) chopped flat-leaf parsley

1 pound (455 g) ground pork

1½ pounds (680 g) lean ground beef

4 slices white bread, crusts removed and chopped into small pieces

¼ cup (60 ml) buttermilk

1 tablespoon (8 g) Cajun Seasoning Blend (page 231)

1 tablespoon (6 g) garlic powder

Kosher salt and freshly ground black pepper

1 cup (100 g) unseasoned bread crumbs

2 cups (60 g) spinach leaves, stems removed

8 slices pepper Jack cheese

1 cup (240 g) red pepper jelly

1 cup (240 g) ketchup

2 (1-pound [455 g]) packages thick-sliced smoked bacon

1. Preheat the oven to 350°F (180°C). Line a baking sheet with foil.

2. In a skillet over medium-high heat, add the oil. Add the onion, celery, and bell pepper and sauté until the onion turns translucent, about 5 minutes. Add the garlic, rosemary, and parsley and cook for another 3 minutes. Remove from the heat and let cool.

3. In a large mixing bowl, add the pork and beef. Add the cooled vegetables to the meat and, using your hands, gently mix. To prevent the fat in the meat from melting at room temperature, place in the refrigerator and chill (about 15 minutes) while you continue prepping.

4. Make a panade by soaking the bread and buttermilk together in a bowl. Squeeze out the excess moisture and break the panade into pieces and distribute evenly into the meat. Add the Cajun seasoning, garlic powder, salt, and pepper. Gradually add the bread crumbs to balance the moisture content of the meat mixture until you have a consistency dry enough to shape into a loaf. Chill in the refrigerator while you continue the prep.

recipe continues

THE BACON WEAVE

The bacon weave technique has been around for a while now, and whoever came up with the idea should be enshrined in the culinary hall of fame. It's a simple process of alternating strips of bacon until you have a basket weave of pork flavor. There are lots of online videos that show you how, and once you see it done, you will (like me) become obsessed with trying it out. And in this Bacon-Wrapped Meat Loaf recipe, it works deliciously.

Make the bacon weave by laying 10 slices of thick-cut bacon vertically on a cutting board, touching one another. Pull every other strip down and lay a slice of bacon horizontally across. Pull up the vertical strips to form the first weave. Pull down alternating slices of bacon and repeat with the horizontal strips until the weave is complete. The bacon weave should be approximately 12 inches (30 cm) across, large enough to cover the meat loaf (use a tape measure to be sure).

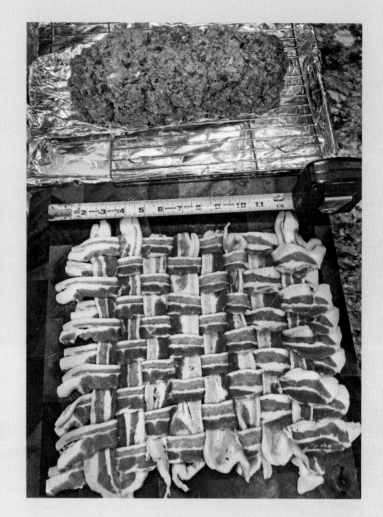

5. Place a metal rack on the prepared baking sheet. Place a sheet of aluminum foil just large enough to hold your meat loaf on the top center of the metal rack. (This will support the meat, but allow the fat to drip into the foil-lined tray below.)

6. Mound half of the meat mixture on the foil and form a base. Layer with spinach leaves and place slices of the cheese on top. Mound the second half of the meat on top and form a loaf. Chill the meat in the refrigerator.

7. In a microwavable bowl, add the pepper jelly and ketchup. Microwave on high for 30 seconds, just until the mixture has softened. Stir to combine.

8. Make the bacon weave (see Sidebar story).

9. Before adding the bacon weave, lightly brush the meat loaf on the top and sides with the ketchup/pepper jelly glaze, reserving some for later use. Using a long spatula,

move the bacon weave over the meat loaf and drape it evenly to cover the top and sides. Tuck the excess under the edges. Add a bit of water to the bottom of the baking sheet to catch any grease.

10. Place the meat loaf in the oven and bake until the internal temperature reaches 160°F (71°C), about 1 hour.

11. Once the meat has cooked through, remove the meat loaf and let it rest for 10 minutes. Just before serving, brush some of the glaze over the bacon and place back in the hot oven. Watch carefully as the glaze sets and the top begins to brown, stopping short of burning. (Note: Black bits equal flavor, but it will burn quickly; 2 minutes maximum is all that is needed.)

12. To serve, place the meat loaf on a platter and garnish with a sprig of rosemary. Place in the center of the table, cut thick slices, and serve with more of the warm glaze on the side.

CHICKEN THIGHS WITH CREOLE JASMINE RICE

To me, the dark meat is the juiciest part of the chicken and retains its flavor long after the breast meat has dried out. I contend that with the right preparation, they become the star attraction on your dinner plate. Tomato-infused Creole jasmine rice is the perfect bed on which to rest these crispy-skin chicken thighs. When the rice is cooked down in stock, it has a small-grain, textural quality that is perfect for this Louisiana recipe.

CREOLE JASMINE RICE

2 cups (320 g) white Louisiana jasmine rice

1 cup (160 g) diced onion

1 tablespoon (8 g) Cajun Seasoning Blend (page 231)

2 cups (480 ml) chicken stock

1½ cups (360 ml) water

1 large tomato, chopped

1 (10-ounce [280 g]) can mild diced tomatoes with green chiles

Kosher salt and freshly ground black pepper

CHICKEN THIGHS

4 bone-in, skin-on chicken leg quarters with thighs

Kosher salt

½ cup (120 ml) chicken stock

½ cup (50 g) diced green onion tops

CREOLE JASMINE RICE

1. In a large pot with a lid over high heat, add the rice, onion, Cajun seasoning, chicken stock, and water. Bring to a boil and immediately reduce the heat to a simmer. Cover the pot and cook undisturbed until the rice is done, about 20 minutes.

2. Turn off the heat, lift the lid, and stir in the chopped fresh tomato and the canned tomatoes. Season with salt and pepper to your taste. Cover and keep warm until serving.

CHICKEN THIGHS

1. Preheat the oven to 400°F (200°C).

2. Using a sharp paring knife, slice around the leg bone about 1 inch (2.5 cm) from the end and peel back the skin and meat. Cut away any tendons. Pull the skin down to the end of the leg bone and, using kitchen shears or a heavy knife, slice off the tip end of the bone. Push up on the rest of the leg meat and expose the bone. Season the chicken pieces lightly with salt.

3. Add the chicken to a cold (not preheated) cast-iron skillet, skin-side down. Weigh down the meat to make maximum surface contact by placing a pan (that is a bit smaller than the diameter of the skillet) on top of the chicken. Add weight to the pan (stacked up cans work well) and push down.

4. Turn the heat to medium and let the chicken cook undisturbed for 20 minutes. You will hear sizzling and see oil leaching from the skin, but do not be tempted to check the chicken.

recipe continues

5. Remove the pan from the heat and, using a metal spatula with a sharp edge, scrape up the chicken pieces along with the crust and fond underneath. Flip them over and inspect that the skin is browned and crispy.

6. Add the chicken stock to the skillet and place in the oven to roast uncovered until the internal temperature of the thickest part of the thigh reaches 165°F (74°C), about 15 minutes. Transfer the chicken pieces to a platter to rest.

7. To serve, add the rice to the cast-iron skillet and lay the chicken on top. Place in the oven long enough to warm through, about 5 minutes. Garnish with the diced green onion.

BUY LOCAL. BUY FRESH.

Buying seafood direct ensures freshness. To find local fishermen, I go to the Louisiana Direct Seafood website (Sources, page 232) for vendor information. When you buy at the supermarket, you take a chance on both quality and local sourcing. Foreign products disguised as local have begun to appear even in Louisiana grocery stores, and it's up to consumers to be smart.

It's good to know what to look for. Fresh shrimp should have the mild smell of fresh sea air. Shells should hold tightly to the flesh, and legs should be intact. Meat should be firm and translucent. Be sure to avoid seafood with any scent of ammonia. Rest assured, nothing tastes better than fresh Louisiana seafood.

THIN-CUT FRIED CATFISH

It's hard to figure out why thin-cut fried catfish is so good, but it just is. In this recipe sweet white catfish fillets are cut into uniform strips, seasoned, and then fried to perfection. While there is just enough moist fish to bite into, there is an equally satisfying crunch that totally redefines the experience of eating catfish. With shoestring French fries, a side of slaw, a touch of tartar sauce, and an ice-cold beer, this might become your favorite fish dish of all time.

5 pounds (2.2 kg) wild catfish fillets

Vegetable, peanut, or canola oil, for frying

3 cups (280 g) yellow cornmeal

1 cup (120 g) all-purpose flour

2 tablespoons (16 g) Cajun Seasoning Blend (page 231)

Salt

1 large lemon, cut into wedges

1. Wash and inspect the catfish fillets, removing any imperfections. Lay a fillet on a raised cutting board. Using a razor-sharp, thin-bladed boning knife, start at the tail end of the fillet and move the knife along the middle, slicing the fish into a long, thin strip. If there is skin attached, slice the meat just above it and discard the skin. Continue until all the fillets are thinly sliced.

2. Add the oil to a deep fryer or large pot to a depth of 4 to 6 inches (10 to 15 cm). Heat to 375°F (190°C) on a fry thermometer.

3. In a large metal mixing bowl, add the cornmeal, flour, and seasoning and whisk to combine. Add a batch of the fish fillets and toss to coat evenly; shake off any excess coating. Add the fish to the hot oil and fry until golden brown; remove to a wire rack over paper towels, and salt immediately. Continue frying quickly in batches until all are fried golden brown (be careful not to overcook).

4. Garnish with lemon wedges and serve immediately.

MIDDENDORF'S—THE HOME OF THIN FRIED CATFISH

To call Middendorf's the mecca of catfish is no overstatement. Folks routinely exit I-10 and I-12 and drive miles out of their way to the tiny fishing village of Manchac for the tastiest catfish around. It all started in 1934 with a $500 loan from a friend, and the dreams of Louis and Josie Middendorf took off. Josie's recipe for thin-cut, crispy fried catfish is still the main attraction on the menu.

NOTES Buy wild catfish if you can find it. If not, inspect your fillets carefully; the flesh should be white and odor-free (be sure to smell it). Partially freezing the fillets makes them easier to cut evenly. The downfall of fried fish is letting it sit around for too long on paper towels to get cold and soggy. I like to fry the fish when my guests are seated at the table, and I serve the fish family-style in batches as it comes out of the fryer.

STUFFED BELL POPPER

Green bell peppers stuffed to the shoulders with ground meat, spicy pepper Jack cheese, and creamy mashed potatoes are good enough on their own, but drape them in smoky bacon glazed with red pepper jelly, and they are otherworldly. This stuffed bell pepper recipe is a take on the ever-popular bacon-wrapped, jalapeño popper that has become ubiquitous on backyard grills.

2 large russet potatoes, peeled and quartered

1 tablespoon (15 ml) kosher salt

1 tablespoon (15 ml) unsalted butter

Freshly ground black pepper

4 extra-large green bell peppers

1 tablespoon (15 ml) olive oil

½ cup (120 ml) diced yellow onion

1 tablespoon (15 ml) minced garlic

1 (10-ounce [280 g]) can mild diced tomatoes and green chiles, drained

1 pound (455 g) ground beef

1 pound (455 g) ground pork

1 medium egg

1 cup (240 ml) unseasoned bread crumbs

1 tablespoon (15 ml) Cajun Seasoning Blend (page 231)

4 slices pepper Jack cheese

8 strips regular smoked bacon

3 tablespoons (45 ml) red pepper jelly

1. In a large pot, add the potatoes. Fill with enough water to cover the potatoes, and season the water with the salt. Over high heat, bring the water to a boil and then reduce to a simmer. Cook for approximately 15 minutes, until the potatoes are fork tender. Drain the water from the potatoes and using a potato ricer, process the potatoes until all lumps are gone. Return the shredded potatoes to the warm pot and stir in butter and a grind of black pepper. Cover the pot and keep warm.

2. Preheat the oven to 400°F (200°C).

3. Slice the bell peppers lengthwise on one side of the stem to the base. Remove these caps and dice them for use in the stuffing mix. Using a paring knife, form a deep cavity in the pepper by removing the inside ribs and seeds. Shake out any remaining seeds.

4. In a large skillet over medium-high heat, add the oil. Once the oil is hot, add the onion, diced bell pepper, and garlic. Sauté just until the onions turn translucent, about 5 minutes. Add the drained tomatoes and continue cooking until the flavors come together, another 5 minutes. Remove the skillet from the heat and let cool (optionally, place the mixture in the refrigerator to expedite cooling).

5. In a large mixing bowl, add the ground meats and the cooled vegetable mixture. Break the egg into the mixture and add the bread crumbs. Using your hands, combine the ingredients so that they mix evenly.

6. In each bell pepper, add enough of the mashed potatoes to cover the bottom. Spoon in some of the meat mixture to fill the pepper cavity nearly to the top, and place pepper Jack cheese on top. Next, mound enough of the remaining meat mixture to encase the cheese and create a dome. Lay strips of bacon on top.

7. Place the peppers onto a foil-lined baking tray with just a bit of water to create steam. Cover the entire tray with a sheet of foil to encase the peppers. Place in the hot oven for 1 hour.

8. Meanwhile, add the pepper jelly to a microwaveable dish with just a teaspoon

of water; microwave on high for about 15 seconds or until the jelly melts. The glaze should now be brushable.

9. Remove the stuffed peppers from the oven, and uncover. Brush the bacon and the top of the meat with the pepper jelly glaze. Return to the oven for another 30 minutes, or until the bacon crisps, the glaze sets, and blackened bits begin to appear. Be careful not to burn.

10. Remove the peppers and serve on individual plates.

NOTES Feel free to buy the individually wrapped, pre-sliced pepper Jack cheese, but if you can only find the block cheese, then slice off in thin chunks to ensure melting. Instead of thick-cut, use the regular sliced bacon so that they will bake crispy. For the ground beef, I usually specify 80/20 ground chuck, but not here; the ground pork will lend enough fat and flavor to the mix.

BLACK DRUM AND SHRIMP

White flaky Gulf fish and jumbo Louisiana shrimp are seasoned and pan-sautéed to crown a bed of greens in this healthy entrée that is lightly dressed with an olive oil and balsamic vinegar combination. I've kept my ingredients basic, but get creative and add ripe tomato, cucumber, avocado, or whatever is fresh and tasty.

4 (6-ounce [168 g]) black drum or favorite fish fillets

8 jumbo (16/20 count) shrimp, peeled, tail on

1 tablespoon (8 g) Cajun Seasoning Blend (page 231)

½ cup (120 ml) extra-virgin olive oil

¼ cup (60 ml) white balsamic vinegar

4 cups (120 g) mixed greens

1 cup (145 g) roasted yellow corn kernels

½ cup (58 g) sliced radish

½ cup (80 g) sliced red onion

2 tablespoons (30 ml) olive oil

Freshly ground black pepper

4 grapefruit segments

4 orange segments

1. Lightly season the fish and the shrimp with Cajun seasoning. Cover and refrigerate until ready to use.

2. In a lidded jar, add the extra-virgin olive oil and balsamic vinegar. Cover and shake well until mixed. Refrigerate until ready to use.

3. In a large mixing bowl add the greens, corn, radish, and onion. Drizzle with olive oil and balsamic vinegar dressing, and toss to coat the ingredients. Cover and refrigerate until ready to use.

4. In a saucepan over medium-high heat, add the 2 tablespoons (30 ml) olive oil. Once sizzling hot, add the fish and cook for 5 minutes. Turn the fish and add the shrimp to the pan. Cook the fish for 2 minutes longer or until done. Turn the shrimp and cook until done, about 3 minutes total.

5. Add the salad mixture to plates and top with a fish fillet and equal portions of the shrimp. Grind fresh cracked pepper over the salad. Garnish with the grapefruit and orange segments. Lightly drizzle the dressing over the fish and serve the remaining dressing on the side.

NOTE Black drum has the sweet taste and flaky texture of redfish. The flash-frozen and vacuum-packed Vermilion Bay Sweet brand of black drum fillets are shipped online by the nonprofit Louisiana Direct Seafood (Sources, page 232), a program of Louisiana Sea Grant and LSU Ag Center.

SKILLET-FRIED QUAIL WITH HONEY HEAT

If asked to name one Southern dish worthy of praise, most folks would say fried chicken. But for me, there's something about the taste of farm-raised quail with its delicate, close-to-the-bone meat hand-battered and fried that ascends to a higher culinary calling. One bite into the spice and crunch of these crispy-skinned, skillet-fried quail will astound you. The sweet meat balanced by honey heat fires on every taste receptor as your guests go back for seconds.

4 whole farm-raised quail, cleaned

2 cups (480 ml) buttermilk

1 tablespoon (15 ml) hot sauce

2 tablespoons (36 g) table salt

½ cup (170 g) honey

½ cup (120 ml) sriracha sauce

Peanut oil, for frying

2 cups (240 g) all-purpose flour

2 tablespoons (16 g) Cajun Seasoning Blend (page 231)

1 tablespoon (8 g) smoked paprika

Kosher salt

1 cup (100 g) diced green onion tops

1. Cut each quail in half down the breastbone and remove the backbone and any protruding portion of the neck. In a covered container, combine the buttermilk, hot sauce, and table salt. Add the quail, stir to combine, cover, and refrigerate for at least 3 hours or overnight.

2. Add the honey and sriracha sauce to a bowl. Stir to combine and keep at room temperature.

3. In a cast-iron pot or skillet over medium-high heat, add enough oil to come halfway up the sides of the pan or at least 3 inches (7.5 cm) deep. Bring the oil to a temperature of 375°F (190°C) on a fry thermometer.

4. Remove the quail from the refrigerator and drain on a wire rack. Add the flour, Cajun seasoning, and paprika to a mixing bowl and whisk to combine. Working in batches, dredge the wet quail halves in the flour and add to the hot oil (do not crowd the pot). Fry until golden brown and done, 8 to 10 minutes each. Drain the quail on a wire rack over a paper towel–lined tray and immediately sprinkle with kosher salt. Drizzle with the honey heat sauce and sprinkle with the green onion. Serve family style in the center of the table with extra sauce on the side.

NOTES When I can, I always buy my quail from a local farmer, but farm-raised quail can be found in the frozen food section and are readily available at most supermarkets or Asian grocers.

FRIED EGGPLANT WITH CRAWFISH ÉTOUFFÉE

Crispy eggplant fried golden brown is a study in textural contrasts. While the crusty exterior crackles with crispness, the inside cooks to a smooth, almost sauce-like creaminess. And when topped with a velvet cloak of rich and spicy crawfish étouffée, this Louisiana recipe is sheer genius.

ÉTOUFFÉE

½ cup (120 g) unsalted butter

1 cup (160 g) diced yellow onion

½ cup (75 g) diced green bell pepper

½ cup (60 g) diced celery

1½ teaspoons minced garlic

1 pound (455 g) Louisiana crawfish tail meat (see Sources, page 232)

1 tablespoon (8 g) all-purpose flour

½ cup (120 ml) seafood stock

½ teaspoon cayenne pepper

Kosher salt and freshly ground black pepper

Dash of hot sauce

EGGPLANT

1 large eggplant

Kosher salt

Peanut oil, for frying

1 cup (120 g) all-purpose flour

1 tablespoon (8 g) Cajun Seasoning Blend (page 231)

1 large egg, beaten

½ cup (120 ml) whole milk

1 teaspoon hot sauce

1 cup (100 g) unseasoned bread crumbs

½ cup (50 g) diced green onion tops

ÉTOUFFÉE

1. In a large cast-iron skillet over medium-high heat, melt the butter. Add the onion, bell pepper, and celery and sauté until the onion turns translucent, about 5 minutes. Add the garlic, lower the heat to a simmer, and stir to combine. Add the crawfish tail meat and stir to combine. Sprinkle the flour over the mixture, stir to incorporate, and add the stock. Stir until the stock thickens into a tight sauce-like consistency, about 5 minutes. Let simmer for 5 minutes longer and then turn off the heat. Season to taste with cayenne pepper, salt, and pepper along with a dash or two of hot sauce. Keep warm until ready to serve.

EGGPLANT

1. Slice the eggplant into 4 rounds of uniform 1-inch (2.5 cm) thickness. Place on a plate lined with paper towels. Sprinkle both sides with salt and place in the refrigerator for at least 1 hour or overnight.

2. In a cast-iron pot or skillet over medium-high heat, add oil to at least 3 inches (7.5 cm) deep. Bring the oil to a temperature of 350°F (180°C) on a fry thermometer.

3. Remove the eggplant from the refrigerator and use paper towels to remove any excess moisture or surface salt.

4. In a shallow bowl, add the flour and seasoning. Stir to combine.

5. In another shallow bowl, add the egg, milk, and hot sauce; whisk to combine.

6. In a third shallow bowl, add the bread crumbs.

7. Dip each eggplant round into the flour; add to the egg mixture; and coat with the bread crumbs.

8. Add the coated eggplant to the hot oil and fry until golden brown on both sides, 5 to 8 minutes. Remove and drain on paper towels. Lightly sprinkle with salt.

9. To serve, place the eggplant rounds on a platter and spoon a generous portion of étouffée over each. Sprinkle with the green onion and serve family style.

NOTES This recipe version of crawfish étouffée is more like a sauce (less liquid) than a true stew-like étouffée. It is best to peel your crawfish, but packaged tail meat (Louisiana, of course) is a huge time-saver and works just fine. If you use the packaged, be sure to add a little water to the fat inside the bag to get out all the flavor.

ROOT BEER-GLAZED PORK BELLY TACOS

Pork belly is a workhorse ingredient in south Louisiana kitchens. Cured and smoked for bacon, brined and pickled for salt pork, or sliced and fried for grattons, the belly of the pig has always been a part of every Louisiana cook's repertoire. But while some cooks have relegated pork belly to a few cultural favorites, the rest of the culinary world has moved it to a center-of-the-plate, star attraction, like this recipe. My pork belly tacos use familiar Louisiana ingredients such as Barq's root beer and Steen's sugarcane molasses in a dish that elevates the taco experience. Marinated, glazed, lacquered, and bronzed, this pork belly turns out moist and meaty with a crackling crust.

PORK BELLY

1 (2½- to 3-pound [1 to 1.4 kg]) pork belly

2 cups (480 ml) apple juice

2 cups (480 ml) root beer soda

2 tablespoons (30 ml) soy sauce

¼ cup (60 ml) Worcestershire sauce

½ cup (170 g) sugarcane molasses, such as Steen's (see Sources, page 232)

1 tablespoon (6 g) ground ginger

1 cup (225 g) packed light brown sugar

1 teaspoon kosher salt

1 teaspoon black pepper

2 sprigs fresh rosemary

2 tablespoons (16 g) cornstarch

2 tablespoons (30 ml) water

TACOS

1 cup (70 g) thinly sliced napa cabbage

2 tablespoons (16 g) julienned carrot

2 tablespoons (16 g) thinly diced celery

1 cup (240 g) mayonnaise

½ cup (120 g) sour cream

2 tablespoons (30 ml) white wine vinegar

1 teaspoon freshly squeezed lemon juice

1 teaspoon Dijon mustard

Kosher salt and freshly ground black pepper

8 flour tortillas

½ cup (120 g) thinly sliced bread and butter pickles

½ cup (50 g) diced green onion tops

PORK BELLY

1. With a sharp knife, score the top fat layer of the pork belly in a crisscross pattern, making sure to stop before penetrating the meat. This allows the marinade to penetrate the meat, the skin to crisp, and the fat to render.

2. In an ovenproof dish, combine the apple juice, root beer, soy sauce, Worcestershire, and molasses. While stirring, add the ginger, sugar, salt, and pepper. Submerge the belly fat-side up in the marinade, add the rosemary sprigs, cover with aluminum foil, and marinate overnight in the refrigerator.

3. Preheat the oven to 375°F (190°C).

4. Remove the dish with the pork belly from the refrigerator and let it come to room temperature. Pour most of the marinade into a saucepan leaving only enough in the dish to immerse the belly about ½ inch (1.3 cm) deep. Cover the dish tightly with aluminum foil and place in the oven. Cook for 3 hours, checking every 30 minutes to make sure there is still enough cooking liquid to prevent burning. Remove from the oven and pour off any remaining cooking liquid into the saucepan. Measure 1 cup (240 ml) and discard the rest.

5. While the pork belly is cooling, make the glaze. Over medium-high heat, bring the saucepan containing the marinade/cooking liquid to a boil and lower the heat to a simmer.

6. In a small bowl, add the cornstarch and water and stir together until the cornstarch dissolves to make a slurry. Pour it into the pot and turn the heat to high. Once the mixture comes to a boil, lower the heat and stir as it thickens enough to coat the back of a spoon. Turn off the heat and keep at room temperature until ready to use.

7. Turn the oven to 450°F (230°C).

8. Brush the glaze generously on the pork belly in the ovenproof dish, making sure to penetrate between the layers of fat. Make sure the pork belly is fat-side up and transfer to the hot oven. Keep a close eye on the meat and watch as the top fat layer begins to bronze and lacquer with the root beer glaze, about 10 minutes. Be careful not to let it burn.

9. Remove from the oven and brush once again with the glaze. Move the belly to a cutting board and slice into bite-size pieces.

TACOS

1. For the slaw and sauce, add the cabbage, carrot, and celery to a mixing bowl. In another mixing bowl, whisk together the mayonnaise, sour cream, vinegar, lemon juice, and mustard. Season to taste with salt and pepper. Add 2 tablespoons (30 ml) of the sauce to the slaw and mix to combine. Pour the remaining sauce into a serving bowl.

2. For the tacos, move the tortillas to a microwavable plate and cover with a damp paper towel. Microwave on high until steaming hot, 1 to 2 minutes. Add a generous portion of slaw to the bottom of the taco and top with several pieces of pork belly. Drizzle with some of the remaining root beer glaze and the white sauce. Garnish with the sliced pickles and green onion. Serve with ice-cold beer.

SMOKED PORK SAUSAGE WITH HATCH CHILES

I look forward to Hatch chiles. They are grown in the Hatch Valley of New Mexico, and for a brief time in late summer (August/September), they flood the markets and are seen throughout Louisiana. With the zing of these chile peppers providing a palate-pleasing backdrop, the smoky sausage brings a wallop of hog flavor that only smoked pork sausage can deliver. Serve with white rice and a side of cornbread.

½ cup (70 g) diced smoked pork jowl bacon or regular bacon

2 pounds (910 g) mild smoked pork sausage or any mild smoked sausage, sliced into bite-size chunks

1 cup (160 g) chopped yellow onion

½ cup (60 g) chopped celery

½ cup (25 g) chopped flat-leaf parsley

½ cup (75 g) chopped red and yellow bell pepper

2 cups (300 g) sliced mild Hatch chile peppers, seeds and membrane removed, or poblano peppers, if not in season

1 tablespoon (8 g) minced garlic

½ cup (60 g) all-purpose flour

2 cups (480 ml) chicken stock, divided

1 teaspoon smoked paprika

2 teaspoons Cajun Seasoning Blend (page 231)

Kosher salt and freshly ground black pepper

6 cups (1.2 kg) cooked long-grain white rice, for serving (optional)

1. In a large cast-iron skillet with a heavy lid over medium-high heat, add the bacon and cook until the fat renders out and the bacon crisps, about 8 minutes. Remove the bacon and all but 1 tablespoon (15 ml) of the grease. Add the sausage and cook until browned on both sides, 5 to 8 minutes, then remove to a platter and keep warm. Add the onion, celery, parsley, bell pepper, and Hatch chiles to the skillet. Cook for 5 minutes or until the chiles begin to brown, and then add the garlic and cook for 1 minute longer.

2. Return the sausage and bacon pieces to the skillet and sprinkle with the flour. Stir the mixture and cook the flour just until the raw taste disappears, about 3 minutes. Add 1½ cups (360 ml) of the chicken stock and reserve the rest if needed. Stir the mixture and bring to a boil. Add the paprika, Cajun seasoning, and a pinch of salt and pepper. Lower the heat to a simmer and cover. Cook for 20 minutes. Uncover and check to see if more stock is needed to achieve a stew-like consistency. Taste the mixture and add salt and pepper if needed. Serve family style in the skillet with a bowl of cooked white rice, if desired.

FIGS AND FLUFF

Late-summer figs are reason enough to put up with the long, hot summer in Louisiana. When it's picking time and the juices are literally oozing from these meaty morsels, I'm there with bushel baskets in hand. And this brilliantly simple, beautifully silky, and oh so sweet recipe is the best way I know to enjoy fresh figs.

12 fresh figs

1 (7-ounce [198.5 g]) box vanilla pizzelle cookies, such as Reko brand, or any flat vanilla cookie

1 (7½-ounce [213 g]) jar marshmallow fluff

½ cup (70 g) crumbled pecans

¼ cup (85 g) local honey

4 sprigs mint

1. Slice the stem end off and cut 8 of the figs in half lengthwise, leaving 4 figs whole. Place on a platter.

2. Place 4 of the pizzelle cookies on a cutting board. Spread the marshmallow fluff generously on top of each all the way to the edge of the cookie. Sprinkle the top of the fluff lightly with the crumbled pecans. Place the fig halves skin-side down on the fluff in a circular pattern with one whole fig standing in the middle of each cookie. Drizzle the honey lightly over the figs.

3. Place the completed pastry onto an individual serving plate. For garnish, take a sprig of mint by the hard stem and poke it into the top of the center fig of each dessert.

LEMON-ROSEMARY RUM COOLER

While a big pitcher of homemade lemonade brings genteel Southern credibility to any backyard gathering, I profess that adding a splash (or two) of rum to the tall glass can only lengthen the slow drawl of the conversation. And clipping fresh sprigs of rosemary to add to the mix brings fragrance to the nose while sipping this glorious cocktail. I love it so.

8 lemons, preferably Meyer lemons

8 sprigs rosemary, divided

9 lemon slices, seeds removed, divided

½ cup (100 g) sugar

Kosher salt

4 (1.5-ounce [45 ml]) jiggers rum, such as Bayou Rum (see Sources, page 232)

1. In a 2-quart (1.8 L) pitcher, squeeze the juice of the lemons, removing any seeds. Add 4 of the rosemary sprigs and 4 slices of the lemon. Add the sugar, fill the pitcher with water, and stir. Let steep for 2 hours or overnight.

2. Using four tall glasses, rub each rim with 1 lemon slice. Invert the glass onto a plate covered with kosher salt and move the rim around the salt until coated.

3. Fill each glass with ice, add 1 jigger of rum, and top with the lemonade. Finish by adding 1 slice of lemon and 1 sprig of rosemary for garnish. Repeat for each cocktail.

MEYER LEMONS

Meyer lemons grow naturally in my backyard, and it seems that every other year I have a bumper crop. Meyer lemons came into culinary popularity in the 1990s thanks to California chef Alice Waters, who introduced them in her first cookbook. I love how this hybrid—a cross between a true lemon and a mandarin–has a distinct flavor versus your average supermarket citrus. More fragrant, I think. Less tart, with a citrus edge that brings a slight grin rather than a sourpuss pucker. These lemons still need sweetness, so be sure to add a bit of granulated sugar (or sugar substitute).

PRALINE CREAM FLOAT WITH SPICED RUM

Ice cream floats have always been a weakness. I remember a simpler time and place sitting at the soda fountain at my neighborhood Rexall drugstore, sipping a root beer float and flipping the pages of the latest Archie comic. Okay, so that was a few long years ago, but the memories linger on. For my retro ice cream float, locally produced Swamp Pop Praline Cream Soda and butter pecan ice cream are the foundation for a splash of spiced rum and a dollop of cinnamon whipped cream. With a sprinkling of chopped Cane River pecans (see Sources, page 232), this Praline Cream Float is a down-home Louisiana classic. This is what sweet memories are made of.

CINNAMON WHIPPED CREAM

½ cup (240 ml) heavy whipping cream

1 teaspoon (8 g) ground cinnamon

1 teaspoon (12 g) sugar

PRALINE CREAM FLOAT

2 scoops butter pecan ice cream or a quality vanilla ice cream

1 (12-ounce [340 ml]) bottle cold Swamp Pop Praline Cream Soda (see Sources, page 232) or cream soda

1 (1.5 ounce [45 ml]) jigger spiced rum, such as Bayou Rum (optional; see Sources, page 232)

1 tablespoon (10 g) chopped pecans

1 sprig mint, for garnish

CINNAMON WHIPPED CREAM

1. In a cold metal mixing bowl, add the cream, cinnamon, and sugar. With an immersion blender or hand mixer, blend the cream on high speed until soft peaks form. Cover and chill before serving.

PRALINE CREAM FLOAT

1. In an ice-cold mug or glass, add the ice cream. Pour over the soda and add the rum. Top with a generous dollop of cinnamon whipped cream and the chopped pecans. Garnish with a sprig of mint.

CHAPTER 3

FALL

AT THE FIRST SIGN OF COOLER AUTUMN WEATHER, the gumbo pots come out and the smokehouses fire up. I love to travel the back roads during this time of year and stop at some of my favorite out-of-the-way places. One October morning, I met T-Boy and learned his secrets.

Paul Berzas, alias T-Boy, has created quite a stir in boudin circles. This mild-mannered Cajun from Mamou, Louisiana, has consistently brought to market one of the most sought-after links in all of Louisiana. His brand of A+ rated (source: Boudinlink.com) boudin has placed first in numerous blind-tasting competitions, edging out some big names in the business.

I had long heard of this legend, and to find out how he did it, I decided to go to the source.

I wasn't sure what to expect, but what I found was a bustling marketplace of shoppers lined up at various counters with armloads of meat products and a hankering for a link of boudin or two for the ride home. When I asked if T-Boy was there, I was sent toward the rear of the store behind the meat counter and what appeared to be the hardest working person in the place.

There was much to learn in this shrine to all things pork, and I had a barrage of questions, starting with boudin. T-Boy is a gracious host and welcomed my prodding for more about his operation. He willingly shared his secrets for his award-winning boudin, and he is not shy about saying how proud he is of helping promote the boudin culture of South Louisiana.

But what T-Boy showed me next was a pork revelation—Jalapeño Pepper Jack Stuffed Tasso Roast.

In all my travels, I've only seen this Cajun specialty done once before. Every sausage maker worth his salt makes his personal brand of pork tasso—chunks of pork shoulder highly seasoned and smoked. But T-Boy trims down his pork shoulder to a small 4-pound (1.8 kg) roast and gives it an added depth of flavor with the introduction of amped-up spice and meaty flavors before he smokes it. T-Boy is looking for tenderness, and he says it is important to cut his pork so the grain of the meat is running in the same direction; that way, it cooks up fork tender after slicing. The stuffing is a combination of his raw pork sausage and thick wedges of pepper Jack cheese with fresh jalapeño slices. He holds it all together with butcher's meat netting, or optionally you can tie it together with twine.

Although the tasso roast you buy from T-Boy is smoked, it is only partially cooked and needs to spend considerable time cooking down to fork tender. For my version, I oven braise my tasso pork roast in a covered cast-iron pot with an onion gravy. In my book, this pork roast—seasoned, smoked, stuffed, and trussed—can only get better with a dark roux–infused onion gravy.

Thank you, T-Boy.

JALAPEÑO PEPPER JACK STUFFED TASSO ROAST

With the first bite of this tender pork roast, smoke and spice flavors flood your taste buds, but then the depth of a peppery cheese stuffing and a dark roux–based onion gravy fill you with comfort. This may be my new favorite fall recipe. Serve with steamed white rice or mashed potatoes.

1 (4-pound [1.8 kg]) pork shoulder roast, trimmed so that the grain runs in the same direction

¾ cup (96 g) Cajun Seasoning Blend (page 231), divided

1 pound (455 g) bulk raw Cajun sausage or Jimmy Dean–style breakfast sausage

4 (1-inch [2.5 cm]-long) wedges pepper Jack cheese

1 large fresh jalapeño, stemmed, seeded, and chopped

1 tablespoon (15 ml) bacon grease

2 large yellow onions, thickly sliced

2 large carrots, peeled and thickly sliced

2 sprigs fresh rosemary

1 cup (140 g) sliced smoked pork sausage

3 cups (720 ml) water

1 tablespoon (15 ml) Dark Cajun Roux (page 230)

1. Prepare an outdoor smoker and set the temperature to 200°F (93°C).

2. Lay the roast on a cutting board and slice open the center lengthwise, forming a large pocket (do not cut all the way through). Sprinkle the inside with half of the Cajun seasoning and stuff the pocket with as much of the raw sausage as will fit. Poke the cheese wedges and jalapeño inside the sausage and seal inside. To hold it together, cover the roast with butcher's netting or tie with twine. Coat the outside of the roast with the rest of the Cajun seasoning. Place in the smoker and smoke for 2 hours.

3. Preheat the oven to 400°F (200°C).

4. In a black iron pot with a heavy lid over medium-high heat, add the bacon grease. Once hot, add the smoked roast and brown on all sides. Add the onions, carrots, rosemary, sausage, and water. Once the water comes to a boil, add the roux. Stir until the roux melts into the cooking liquid, about 5 minutes. Cover the pot and move to the hot oven. Cook for 2 hours.

5. Remove the pot and uncover, moving the roast to a deep serving platter. Carve the roast against the grain into thick slices. Remove the stems from the rosemary sprigs, arrange the carrot chunks around the roast, and pour the onion gravy onto the platter.

BBQ SHRIMP

In this easy recipe, Gulf shrimp are bathed in a buttery mix of herbs and spices that soak into every crevice of the crustacean. The heads are mandatory, as they do the work of sucking up the peppery flavors of the butter sauce and mixing with their natural head fat into some kind of ethereal nectar of the gods. Slurping is not only allowed but guaranteed.

3 pounds (1.4 kg) colossal (9/12 count) Gulf shrimp, head on and shell on

1½ cups (360 g) unsalted butter

1 teaspoon Cajun Seasoning Blend (page 231)

¼ cup (24 g) garlic powder

¼ cup (32 g) finely ground black pepper

¼ cup (60 ml) Worcestershire sauce

¼ cup (60 ml) dry white wine

2 tablespoons (6 g) chopped fresh rosemary

1 tablespoon (3 g) dried oregano, preferably Mexican or Greek

1 tablespoon (6 g) freshly grated lemon zest

Juice of 1 large lemon

1. Preheat the oven to 375°F (190°C).

2. Rinse the shrimp, but dry them with meticulous attention to detail. Water is your enemy. Drain all moisture off the shrimp and lay them out on a dish towel to soak up any water. Then use wads of paper towels to hand-dry the shrimp. If you don't (and I warned you), your butter sauce will be watered down and lose the impact needed for the full taste experience.

3. In large cast-iron skillet or baking dish over medium-high heat, add the butter. As the butter begins to melt, add the Cajun seasoning, garlic powder, black pepper, Worcestershire, wine, rosemary, oregano, lemon zest, and lemon juice. Stir to combine, then add the shrimp. Baste the shrimp with the sauce and place in the hot oven.

4. Bake until the shrimp turn pink and are done, about 30 minutes, basting the shrimp with the butter sauce halfway through. Remove and test the largest shrimp for doneness. If done, serve immediately by placing in the center of the table with lots of French bread.

NOTES Instead of coarsely ground black pepper, use standard pepper; it mixes into the sauce better. And the same can be said for the garlic powder versus fresh garlic. Be vigilant: Overcooking the shrimp will make them hard to peel.

THE ORIGIN OF BBQ SHRIMP

First things first, it's barbecue shrimp but not barbecued. In fact, this recipe never even comes close to a grill or a smoker. As confusing as that important point is, in just five decades, barbecue shrimp has become a New Orleans culinary legend. What started out in 1954 as a courtesy to an out-of-town customer at Pascal's Manale restaurant, on Napoleon Avenue in the uptown area of New Orleans, has taken on legendary status. Not only is it a must-order for every tourist visiting the Big Easy, but it is also equally adored by locals. Recipes abound, and other than the original Manale standard, no two recipes are alike. That said, there is one basic rule: butter, lots of butter.

KALE, BLACK-EYES, AND PORK JOWL SOUP

Soulful simplicity. Stewing down a pot of black-eyes is the foundation, then you'll infuse it with garden-fresh kale, the soul-food flavors of smoky pork jowl, and an intense dark chicken stock. It is a bowl full of warmth to take the chill off the first blast of autumn air as Louisiana heads into fall. Serve with hot cornbread.

3 strips thick-cut smoked pork jowl bacon or regular bacon, diced

1 cup (160 g) diced yellow onion

1 cup (120 g) diced celery

½ cup (75 g) diced red bell pepper

½ cup (75 g) diced green bell pepper

1 cup (120 g) diced carrot

2 tablespoons (16 g) minced garlic

1 cup (175 g) chopped tomatoes

8 cups (1.9 L) dark chicken stock

1 smoked ham hock

2 bay leaves

1 (16-ounce [455 g]) package dried black-eyed peas (not necessary to soak)

1 large bunch of kale, stems removed and chopped

Kosher salt and freshly ground black pepper

1. In a heavy pot with a lid over medium-high heat, add the pork jowl and sauté. Once the meat begins to brown and the fat is rendered, about 8 minutes, add the onion, celery, bell peppers, and carrot. Continue to stir until the onions turn translucent, about 5 minutes. Add the garlic and tomatoes, and continue stirring the ingredients for another 3 minutes.

2. Add the stock, smoked hock, and bay leaves. Stir the black-eyes into the pot and add the kale. Bring the pot to a boil and then quickly decrease the heat to a simmer. Cover and cook for 1 hour.

3. Lift the lid, taste the liquid, and add salt and pepper to taste. Remove the bay leaves and bones of the hock.

4. Serve in large bowls.

ANDOUILLE SAUSAGE AND WHITE BEAN SOUP

Bean there, done that! I cook a lot with beans of all kinds—red, black, green, or white, I love 'em all. Basic bean recipes are cornerstones of our culinary heritage; Louisiana home cooks know their way around a bean pot. Just think about it: tender white limas infused with smoky andouille sausage slowly simmer until they burst, releasing their starch to thicken the pot. Warming your hands cradling a creamy bowl of this soup is the essence of comfort. Serve with toasted French bread rounds.

2 tablespoons (30 ml) bacon grease

1 cup (160 g) diced yellow onion

½ cup (60 g) diced celery

1 cup (120 g) diced carrot

1 (16-ounce [455 g]) package smoked andouille sausage (see Sources, page 232), chopped into bite-size pieces

1 pound (455 g) dried large white beans

6 cups (1.4 L) chicken stock

1 bay leaf

½ cup (25 g) chopped flat-leaf parsley

2 tablespoons (6 g) chopped fresh rosemary

½ teaspoon cayenne pepper

Kosher salt and freshly ground black pepper

Hot sauce, if needed

1. In a large cast-iron pot with a lid over medium-high heat, add the bacon grease and sauté the onion until translucent, about 5 minutes. Add the celery, carrot, and sausage and cook for 5 minutes. Add the beans and enough stock to cover. Add the bay leaf, parsley, and rosemary, and season with cayenne and a sprinkle of salt and pepper. Bring to a boil, and then lower the heat to a simmer. Cover the pot and cook, stirring every 15 minutes to check to see if more stock is needed. Continue cooking until the beans are tender, about 1 hour total.

2. Once the beans are done and the soup is creamy, turn off the heat, remove the bay leaf, taste the soup, and adjust the seasoning accordingly by adding salt, pepper, and hot sauce, if needed.

CAJUN BEER-BOILED PEANUTS

In a nutshell, boiling peanuts is foolproof. And with my slow cooker method, boiling peanuts is dead simple—water, a little salt, and peanuts in a long, slow simmer. From there, the seasoning variations are endless and that's where the fun begins. This Cajun recipe is about spice, not heat, and I have a secret ingredient—beer.

3 pounds (1.4 kg) freshly harvested raw peanuts or dried green peanuts

3 whole heads garlic

3 (12-ounce [360 ml]) bottles beer

6 cups (1.5 L) water, plus more if needed

3 tablespoons (18 g) garlic powder

3 tablespoons (18 g) onion powder

3 tablespoons (18 g) red pepper flakes

1 tablespoon (18 g) table salt

1. Rinse the peanuts and remove any grit or dirt.

2. In the insert of a 6- to 8-quart (5.4 to 7.2 L) slow cooker, add the peanuts. Without peeling them, place the whole heads of garlic in the cooker and pour over the beer. Add enough water to cover the peanuts. Add the garlic powder, onion powder, red pepper flakes, and salt. Stir to combine.

3. Set the timer on the cooker for 10 hours and let cook on low all day or overnight. Test for doneness and cook longer until the peanuts are tender. Add more water to the cooker if needed and set to warm. Let the peanuts soak in the warm liquid for another 2 hours. Serve the peanuts from the cooker and refrigerate any leftovers in a covered container. These boiled peanuts are excellent cold or can be reheated in the slow cooker.

BOILED PEANUTS JUST AHEAD

I travel extensively throughout the South. Taking to the open road and driving along the two-lane, kudzu-blanketed byways of the American South is a treat for me. I guess it stems from all those family summer vacations of old—pajama-clad and packed in the station wagon heading out at the break of dawn to visit the Great Smoky Mountains, and everything in between.

I remember those trips and I vividly recall where every pecan divinity-laced Stuckey's roadside stop was located between my house in Bogalusa, Louisiana, and Rock City, Tennessee. Back in the 1950s and early 1960s, before the Interstate Highway System effectively erased the beauty and mystery of traveling by car, there was a colorful world out there. For the price of a 25-cent gallon of gas, you could barrel along the back roads, and around each curve or at the bottom of every hill there was the prospect of a delicious discovery.

Today, it's "McDonald's Next Exit." Back then, it was "Boiled Peanuts Just Ahead." As soon as you hit Mississippi and all through Alabama, Georgia, and into Tennessee, there was an endless procession of boiled peanut outposts. Some were behind the counter of the country store or next to the register inside the gas station, but just as many were sold roadside out of the back of a pickup.

These were hardworking families with a dream and a sack of goobers. Just a washtub and a wood fire were all that was needed to set up shop along the red clay roadways of the South. A quarter for a bag of salt-infused boiled peanuts was a bargain and would get you down the road until the next stop.

Though times have changed, boiled peanuts are still a summer obsession for most dyed-in-the-wool Southerners, me included. On a recent road trip across the Southeast with Roxanne and our daughter Lauren, we decided to get off the interstates and take to the back roads in search of that long-lost American South that I remember so well. And good news: it's still there, boiled peanuts included. As we traveled through our neighboring states, we looked for them anywhere and found them most everywhere.

But there's a twist: Cajun-spiced peanuts are all the rage, and you'll be hard-pressed not to find a Louisiana version just about anywhere in the Southeast. And not to be outdone by my hillbilly brethren, I have a spiked-up recipe to share with you.

TASSO CHILI CHEESE DIP

When you make this smoky, cheesy, beer-infused dip, it will catapult your cooking cred to new heights. This Louisiana-inspired recipe starts off with—what else?—a roux. Yeah, bacon grease and masa corn flour is the perfect intersect of Cajun and Hispanic flavors. Spice-cured tasso ham is a Louisiana component that adds depth of smokehouse flavor. A hearty craft beer with a sweet, malty aroma and the distinct taste of hops adds flavor, and Chipotle chiles (smoke-dried jalapeños) with their adobo sauce layers on extra smoke and spice. Just add the cheese, and your friends will beg for the recipe.

1 tablespoon (15 ml) bacon grease

3 tablespoons (30 g) masa flour

½ cup (80 g) diced yellow onion

1 (12-ounce [360 ml]) bottle full-bodied beer

1½ cups (210 g) chopped tasso (see Sources, page 232) or smoked ham, divided

2 canned chipotle peppers, chopped, plus 2 tablespoons (30 ml) adobo sauce

1 medium fresh jalapeño pepper, seeded and diced

½ cup (8 g) chopped fresh cilantro

1 (10-ounce [280 g]) can diced tomatoes and green chiles

1 tablespoon (8 g) chili powder

1 teaspoon ground cumin

1 tablespoon (8 g) Cajun Seasoning Blend (page 231)

1½ cups (180 g) grated pepper Jack cheese

1½ cups (180 g) cubed Velveeta cheese

Freshly ground black pepper

Dash of hot sauce (optional)

1 cup (120 g) shredded Oaxaca cheese

½ cup (50 g) chopped green onion tops

Tortilla chips, for serving

1. In a 10-inch (25 cm) cast-iron skillet over medium heat, add the bacon grease and masa flour. While whisking, cook until the flour just begins to turn brown, and then add the onion. Stir until the onion turns translucent, about 5 minutes.

2. Add the beer and stir as the mixture thickens. Add 1 cup (140 g) of the tasso along with the chipotles, adobo sauce, jalapeño, cilantro, and diced tomatoes.

3. Season with the chili powder, cumin, and Cajun seasoning.

4. Add the pepper Jack and Velveeta cheeses, lower the heat to a simmer, and continue stirring until it melts, about 5 minutes. Season with a grind of black pepper and a dash of hot sauce to taste. Just before serving, top the skillet with the remaining ½ cup (70 g) tasso and the shredded Oaxaca cheese, and let melt, about 5 minutes. Garnish with the green onions. Serve in the skillet with warm tortilla chips.

BRAISED COLLARDS IN HOCK STOCK

For me, this is soul food at its best, and cozying up to a steaming bowl of collards is a deep dive into the roots of Southern cooking that are forever entwined with my humble heritage. Smoked meat is the key, and in the smokehouses of South Louisiana, smoked ham hocks are easy to find. The meat clings close to the bone until it lets go of its flavor and infuses the smoky essence of a good stock. I'm amazed by how much meat is on a pork hock, and after picking the chunks away from the bones, you have a mound of smoked ham to add to the greens. Serve with chow chow relish.

5 pounds (2.3 kg) meaty smoked ham hocks (about 12)

1½ pounds (680 g) pig's feet (2 or 3), cut into segments and washed

2 large yellow onions, peeled and quartered

1 garlic bulb

2 bay leaves

6 bunches collard greens

¼ cup (60 g) pork fat (reserved from the stock)

2 cups (320 g) chopped yellow onion

1 tablespoon (18 g) salt

Cornbread, for serving

Hot sauce, for serving

1. Wash the ham hocks and rinse off any seasoning. Place in a large stockpot along with the pig's feet, quartered onions, the whole garlic bulb, and bay leaves. Add water to cover or to come halfway up the sides of your stockpot; a little over 1 gallon (3.6 L) is ideal. Turn the burner on low and let the stock simmer for 8 hours.

2. Turn off the heat and let cool. Strain off the stock into a container with a tight-fitting lid; you should have about 1 gallon (3.6 L) of stock. Place it in the refrigerator overnight. Pick the meat from the bones and discard any fat or gristle. Reserve the meat for use later.

3. The next day, remove the container of stock from the refrigerator and use a large spoon to carefully remove the fat cap from the top of the stock. Reserve ¼ cup (60 g) of the fat and discard the rest. Place the stock back into the refrigerator.

4. Wash the collards in cold water, removing any dirt. Cut off the woody ends. Working in rolled-up batches, slice the greens into 1-inch (2.5 cm) strips.

5. In a large pot or Dutch oven with a heavy lid over medium-high heat, add the reserved pork fat. Add the chopped onion and sauté until translucent, about 5 minutes. Add the greens and stir them into the onions until they begin to wilt. Add the salt and the reserved smoked ham hock meat.

6. Remove the stock from the refrigerator. With the release of collagen in the bones, the hock stock should now be congealed to the texture of gelatin, which is a sign of its velvety richness. You do not have to heat the stock before adding it; just spoon it in and watch it melt into the pot. Add half the stock, and reserve the rest to add as the liquid reduces. Lower the heat to a simmer, cover the pot, and braise the greens until tender, about 2 hours. Add more stock as needed during cooking.

7. Serve in bowls with cornbread and hot sauce on the side.

NOTES While some cooks like to add heat and sweet to the greens with red pepper, sugar, vinegar, and other spices, I believe the potlikker should key on the flavor of the meat and greens; serve the hot sauce and chow chow at the table for those who like it spiked up.

COLLARDS: THE SOUL OF SOUTHERN COOKING

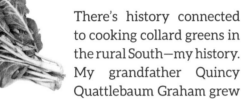

There's history connected to cooking collard greens in the rural South—my history. My grandfather Quincy Quattlebaum Graham grew collards on a piece of dirt in Newton County in central Mississippi. Tucked away on a back-forty acre among the cotton plantations of the region, he farmed the fertile soil and always said that when times got tough, cotton wouldn't fill your belly. He loved collards; he praised them, and he braised them, just as I do over a hundred years later.

My grandfather died before I was born, so for me, cooking collards is a reconnection to the heritage of my family roots. And the key to cooking collards that my father taught me is this: a long, slow braise with the flavor of smoked meat and a minimum of spice (onions and a sprinkle of salt only) to preserve the potlikker. As a son of the South, I learned at an early age that potlikker (or pot liquor), the natural juices and braising liquids that are culinary gold, is the prize of any pot of greens (beans, too). My daddy would load up a bowl with a chunk of cornbread on top, and I would watch him soak up that exalted elixir.

Slowly simmered in a rich broth of smoked ham bones, my braised collards are a journey to the heart of Southern cooking.

SAVORY MIRLITON MUFFINS

Just one bite of these light, herb-filled savory muffins will awaken you to the depth of flavor hiding in the unique vegetable called mirliton. These squash-based muffins bake up easy and cheesy, with crusty outer edges encasing the moist, all-natural flavor within.

2 medium-size mirlitons

1 cup (160 g) diced onion

½ cup (50 g) diced green onion tops

1 tablespoon (3 g) chopped fresh thyme

2 tablespoons (6 g) chopped flat-leaf parsley

1 cup (120 g) grated Cheddar cheese

1½ cups (150 g) bread crumbs

4 large eggs

½ teaspoon Cajun Seasoning Blend (page 231)

1 teaspoon kosher salt

2 teaspoons freshly ground black pepper

1. Preheat the oven to 400°F (200°C). Coat a muffin pan with nonstick spray.

2. Slice the stem ends off the mirlitons; using a box grater, grate both of them. Wrap the grated mirliton in a square of cheesecloth and squeeze out all the moisture. Measure out 2 cups (300 g) of the packed mirliton and place in a large mixing bowl.

3. Add the onion, green onion, thyme, parsley, cheese, and bread crumbs. Break the eggs into the mixture and combine, equally distributing all the ingredients. Season with the Cajun seasoning, salt, and pepper.

4. Spoon the mixture into the cups of the muffin pan. Press down on the tops, compacting the ingredients and filling each cup. Bake in the oven until the tops just begin to brown and the muffins are firm to the touch, about 30 minutes. Remove from the oven and let cool.

5. Invert the muffin pan, tap the sides, and the mirliton muffins should release. If not, run a sharp knife around the inside of the tin until they release. Serve warm or at room temperature.

CHARRED BRUSSELS AU GRATIN

For me, the key to cooking Brussels is to char them until blackened around the edges. The nutty notes will perfume your kitchen and will eliminate the cabbage-type smell that turns off most Brussels sprout haters. Oh yeah, this side dish just took center stage.

2 pounds (910 g) Brussels sprouts

6 strips smoked bacon, chopped

1 cup (160 g) diced yellow onion

1 cup (120 g) diced celery

1 cup (150 g) diced green bell pepper

1 teaspoon minced garlic

1 apple, peeled, cored, and diced (optional)

1 teaspoon fresh thyme

½ teaspoon ground nutmeg

½ teaspoon white pepper

½ teaspoon onion powder

½ cup (120 ml) chicken stock

1 cup (240 ml) heavy whipping cream

1 cup (150 g) cubed Brie cheese, rind removed, divided

Salt and freshly ground black pepper

¼ cup (60 ml) grated mozzarella

1. Remove the woody stem end of each sprout. Cut each sprout in half lengthwise. Reserve for later use.

2. In a large skillet with a lid over medium-high heat, add the bacon and sauté until crispy, about 8 minutes. Remove the bacon and drain on a paper towel.

3. Add the Brussels sprouts to the remaining bacon grease and cook until blackened around the edges, about 10 minutes. Add the onion, celery, bell pepper, and garlic and cook for 3 minutes longer.

4. Add the apple (if using), thyme, nutmeg, white pepper, and onion powder and stir to combine.

5. Add the chicken stock, lower the heat to a simmer, cover the pan, and cook until the stock has evaporated and the sprouts are tender, about 10 minutes.

6. Add the cream and ½ cup (75 g) of the Brie cheese. Cook until the cream reduces and thickens to coat the back of a spoon, about 5 minutes. Season to taste with salt and black pepper. Add the crispy bacon pieces.

7. Divide the mixture among four individual ovenproof ramekins. Insert chunks of the remaining ½ cup (75 g) Brie into the mixture. Sprinkle each with the grated mozzarella.

8. Place the ramekins on a baking sheet and bake under the broiler until bubbly and just beginning to brown on top.

9. Remove and serve immediately.

BLACK-EYED PEA JAMBALAYA

Like many Cajun family cooks, my mother-in-law Rosalie Fontenot Waldrop has collected Cajun recipes all her life, and this handwritten one for Black-Eyed Pea Jambalaya, with its torn edges and ink-smudged words, brings special memories to her. Intrigued by this old-school Louisiana recipe, I was spurred to pull out my vintage rice cooker to see just how easy this dish could be. I was pleasantly surprised at not only the convenience of the cooking method but also the ease of the prep. And it turned out to be a well-balanced dish—flavorful and hearty, with just enough spice to tickle my Cajun taste buds.

1 tablespoon (15 g) unsalted butter

1 cup (160 g) finely chopped yellow onion

1 teaspoon minced garlic

1 tablespoon (3 g) chopped flat-leaf parsley

1½ pounds (680 g) raw Cajun green onion pork sausage or any raw pork sausage, casings removed

2 (15.5-ounce [434 g]) cans black-eyed peas, undrained

1 (10-ounce [280 g]) can mild diced tomatoes and green chiles, drained

1 teaspoon Cajun Seasoning Blend (page 231)

1 teaspoon kosher salt

1 teaspoon freshly ground black pepper

2 cups (480 ml) chicken stock

2½ cups (414 g) raw long-grain white rice

½ cup (50 g) chopped green onion tops, for garnish

Hot sauce, if needed

1. In the insert of an electric rice cooker, add all the ingredients except the green onions and hot sauce, which will be used to garnish and season the finished dish. Stir to combine all the ingredients and make sure the rice and sausage are distributed throughout. Set the timer following the rice cooker instructions, and let cook. When the timer signals that the rice is ready, do not open the lid. Let the cooker continue to steam on warm for another 30 minutes to bring all the flavors of the dish together.

2. Open the lid and gently stir the jambalaya. Do not overstir or it will become gummy. Serve in bowls and garnish with a sprinkle of chopped green onion. Serve hot sauce on the side.

NOTES Be sure to use canned black-eyed peas since dried peas will take much longer to cook than the rice. I do not drain the canning liquid before adding; I like how the added flavor absorbs into the rice. Get creative: Instead of sausage, ground meat would work great in this dish, and a variation using red beans would be an interesting Cajun combination. Don't over-stir this dish once cooked at the risk of it becoming gummy. Store any leftovers in the rice cooker, and, when you reheat, just add a bit of water to steam the rice mixture.

THE ELECTRIC RICE COOKER

It's no secret that Cajun cooks love their black iron skillets, dutch ovens, and propane crawfish cookers. Those are standard-issued items in any Acadiana family's arsenal of kitchen equipment. But, there's one more that is essential: the electric rice cooker.

In rural Cajun kitchens, rice is a centerpiece of the dinner table, and this portable appliance has become indispensable. Even today, when a young Cajun girl plans her wedding, an electric rice cooker is at the top of the gift registry list. It's not unusual to see two rice cookers steaming away during a Sunday dinner. But this wasn't always the case, and it took the foresight of an industrious Cajun in Ville Platte, Louisiana to introduce the rice cooker to Acadiana.

As the story goes, rice cookers became all the rage in the early 1960s because of the efforts of one man, legendary music pioneer Floyd Soileau. Realizing the enormous consumption of rice in Cajun homes, he introduced the Hitachi rice cooker for sale in his Floyd's Record Shop in Ville Platte. It soon caught on, and every Cajun cook made the trek to his store to buy one of the newfangled cookers. In fact, tens of thousands were sold, so many that the president of Hitachi Corporation flew from Tokyo, Japan, to the tiny town of Ville Platte just to find out why more of his products

were being sold there than any other single location in the world.

SMOKED SAUSAGE AND QUAIL JAMBALAYA

This jambalaya is Louisiana roots cooking at its best. The juices mingle in the rice, the sausage absorbs the flavors, and the quail provides a bone-gnawing contrast of tastes. Give this dish a try and see how it delivers on flavor.

4 whole quail, cleaned and partially deboned

1 tablespoon (8 g) Cajun Seasoning Blend (page 231)

4 strips smoked bacon, chopped

2 cups (320 g) diced onion

2 cups (240 g) diced celery

2 cups (300 g) diced green bell pepper

2 tablespoons (16 g) minced garlic

½ cup (120 ml) beer

2 cups (280 g) sliced smoked pork sausage, cut into bite-size pieces

1 cup (50 g) chopped flat-leaf parsley

1 cup (100 g) diced green onion tops

1 tablespoon (8 g) cayenne pepper

Dash of hot sauce

Kosher salt and freshly ground black pepper

4 cups (660 g) uncooked Louisiana long-grain white rice

4 cups (960 ml) chicken stock

1. Preheat the oven to 400°F (200°C).

2. Rinse and dry the quail. Using a sharp knife, cut the quail in half vertically down the middle. Sprinkle the halves with the Cajun seasoning.

3. In a large, heavy cast-iron pot with a heavy lid over medium-high heat, fry the bacon until crispy, about 8 minutes. Remove the bacon pieces and set aside.

4. Add the onion, celery, and bell pepper to the bacon drippings. Cook until the onion is translucent, about 5 minutes, and then add the garlic. Cook for another 2 minutes and then remove the vegetables to a platter.

5. In the same pot, add the quail and sauté until the meat turns brown, about 10 minutes. Deglaze the pot by pouring in the beer and scraping the bits from the bottom of the pot while stirring.

6. Add the sausage, bacon pieces, all of the browned vegetables, parsley, and green onions. Add the cayenne, hot sauce, salt, and pepper to taste.

7. Add the rice to the pot and stir until evenly distributed. Add the stock and stir again.

8. Here is the important part of jambalaya cooking: cover the pot and place in the hot oven for 1 hour. Open a cold beer and forget about it. Do not stir or even raise the lid on the pot for the first hour. In that hour, all the flavors come together, the quail becomes tender, and the rice gently cooks.

9. At the end of 1 hour, take a peek, but do not stir (or it will become sticky and starchy). Taste to see if the rice is cooked to at least al dente. If so, turn off the oven, cover the pot, and let it continue cooking in the carryover heat of the oven for another 20 minutes.

10. When your guests are seated, remove the pot from the oven and place in the middle of the table. Uncover and dig in.

WILD CATFISH FILLETS IN SATSUMA-LEMON MEUNIÈRE SAUCE

Wild catfish is the center of this recipe that features a glaze of citrus butter with floral notes of white wine and rosemary along with the contrast of toasted pecans—a classic Louisiana combination. Oh yeah, we're letting the proverbial cat out of the bag with this recipe.

4 (6- to 8-ounce [168 to 227 g]) wild Louisiana catfish fillets

Kosher salt and freshly ground black pepper

1 cup (120 g) all-purpose flour

1 tablespoon (8 g) Cajun Seasoning Blend (page 231)

½ cup (120 g) unsalted butter

2 tablespoons (30 ml) olive oil

1 cup (140 g) pecan halves

1 tablespoon (3 g) chopped fresh rosemary

1 tablespoon (8 g) minced garlic

1 cup (130 g) freshly peeled satsuma, mandarin, or tangerine segments

1 tablespoon (15 ml) freshly squeezed lemon juice

4 lemon slices, seeds removed

¼ cup (60 ml) dry white wine

1. Remove the fish from the package and trim any thin tail ends of the fillets so that they are of equal size and thickness. Sprinkle lightly with salt and pepper. Place the flour in a shallow pan and stir in the Cajun seasoning. Lightly dust the fillets on all sides with the flour and shake off any excess.

2. In a large skillet over medium-high heat, add the butter and olive oil and bring to a sizzle. Add the fish and cook until browned on both sides, about 8 minutes. Remove from the skillet and keep warm.

3. With the remaining butter/oil in the skillet, place over medium-high heat, and scrape any browned bits from the bottom of the pan. Add the pecans, rosemary, garlic, satsuma, lemon juice, and lemon slices. Bring to a simmer and let cook for 5 minutes. Add the wine and cook until the sauce reduces by half, about 5 minutes. Sample the sauce and season to taste with salt and pepper.

4. Add the catfish fillets back to the pan, and spoon over the sauce to coat. Let cook for 3 minutes longer and serve immediately.

WILD CATS

Throughout the South, a stampede of interest in catfish took off in the 1970s with farmers flooding fields and bringing pond-raised fish to market. While profitable for a decade or so, this aquaculture bonanza was short-lived as the cost of fuel, feed, and labor coupled with an over-supply brought the industry to a screeching halt. And just when farmers thought they had a whisker of a chance to make money, the invasion of cheap, frozen catfish (basa or swai) flooded the market. These days, there's plenty of catfish to go around but sourcing locally caught fish has become more challenging.

Wild catfish are a culinary prize worth seeking. Channel cats, blues, and even flatheads are fished, netted, and noodled by those hungry for the taste of catfish. It's not uncommon to see folks lining the banks with hook and line in hand, or diving in the fresh-water ponds and bayous to hand-catch large 40 pounders. In the Atchafalaya Basin swamp, the Indian technique of hoop nets is the ticket for a mess of wild cats. Both recreational and commercial fishing assures a steady stream of wild catfish coming to the table. The taste is different: cleaner to the palate, with a more pronounced rich, buttery flavor.

HERE ARE THE KEYS: You've got to find a reliable supplier and trust that what you are getting is fresh and wild. Buy it already filleted (you don't want to spend time skinning catfish), and opt for the smaller catfish that has sweeter flesh and ensures that the fish will cook evenly. If your fillets are larger, trim them before cooking.

Louisiana Direct Seafood (Sources, page 232) has a wild-caught catfish product available for purchase on their website. Caught by fisherman Butch Smith of Fresh Water Seafood in Loreauville,

SMOTHERED TURKEY NECKS

This is not a timid dish. Its very design grabs your full attention as you ascend—no, dive—into the dark depths of its culinary abyss. The smoky, bony knobs of neck meat render tender with a moistness that makes them burst with earthy flavor. The tantalizing taste of your first bite will linger long and call you back to the bowl for just one more bite. It's that good—bone-suckin' good.

¼ cup (60 ml) vegetable oil

2 cups (320 g) diced yellow onion

2 cups (300 g) diced green bell pepper

2 cups (240 g) diced celery

2 tablespoons (16 g) minced garlic

½ cup (25 g) chopped flat-leaf parsley

24 smoked turkey necks, about 4 inches (10 cm) long

2 pounds (910 g) smoked pork sausage, cut into 1-inch (2.5 cm) pieces

3 quarts (2.8 L) chicken stock, plus water if needed

1 tablespoon (8 g) cayenne pepper

1 cup (240 ml) Dark Cajun Roux, plus more if needed (page 230)

¼ cup (30 g) cornstarch mixed with ¼ cup (60 ml) cold water (optional)

Kosher salt and freshly ground black pepper

Dash of hot sauce

8 cups (1.6 kg) cooked long-grain white rice, for serving

Filé powder, for serving

1 cup (100 g) diced green onion tops

1. In a large cast-iron pot with a lid over medium-high heat, add the oil. Once sizzling hot, add the onion, bell pepper, and celery. Sauté until the onion turns translucent, about 5 minutes. Add the garlic and parsley and stir until combined. Add the turkey necks and sausage and sauté just until all the vegetables begin to brown, about 8 minutes. Add enough chicken stock to the pot to cover all the turkey necks and vegetables, and scrape the bottom to loosen the brown bits of flavor.

2. Season with cayenne and stir to combine. Add the roux and stir. Bring the pot to a boil and then lower the heat to a simmer. Cover the pot and let it cook for 1 hour.

3. Uncover the pot and skim the surface of any excess oil. Taste and if you prefer it thicker, make a slurry with the cornstarch and cold water and add to the pot. Stir until the desired level of thickness. Add salt and pepper to taste. Cover the pot and simmer for 30 minutes longer.

4. Sample the finished gumbo and season with hot sauce to taste. Serve the gumbo over rice with a sprinkling of filé powder and a shower of diced green onion.

PREP TIME: 30 MINUTES
COOK TIME: 2 HOURS 30 MINUTES
TOTAL TIME: 3 HOURS

BLACK POT BEEF TONGUE WITH GARLIC GRAVY

I once judged the St. Landry Parish Cattlemen's Association Beef Cook-Off, and the hands-down winner was a black pot of simmering beef tongue. The judges sampled every cut of beef imaginable: round steak, oxtail, seven steak, short ribs, rib eye, and tenderloin, to name a few, but when it came time to award the Best of Show winner, beef tongue was all anyone could talk about.

This beef tongue dish adorns rural Cajun and Creole kitchen tables throughout Louisiana. With a prepped beef tongue, the cooking method is quite easy, much akin to pot roast. It must be cleaned and skinned by a professional butcher or an experienced cook and then slowly cooked in a black-iron pot. The tender meat and rich garlic-infused gravy will have your guests coming back for seconds.

1 (2- to 3-pound [910 to 1365 g]) beef tongue, cleaned and skinned

2 tablespoons (30 ml) vegetable oil, divided

2 tablespoons (16 g) Cajun Seasoning Blend (page 231)

1 teaspoon kosher salt

1 teaspoon freshly ground black pepper

1 large yellow onion, sliced

4 ribs celery, diced

2 tablespoons (6 g) chopped fresh rosemary

4 cups (960 ml) beef stock

1 head garlic

¼ cup (30 g) cornstarch mixed with ¼ cup (60 ml) cold water (optional)

2 sprigs rosemary, for garnish

8 cups (1.6 kg) cooked long-grain white rice, for serving

1. Preheat the oven to 400°F (200°C).

2. Move the beef tongue to a cutting board and inspect that the butcher has removed the outer skin. Pat the meat dry and rub it with 1 tablespoon (15 ml) of the oil. Sprinkle evenly with the Cajun seasoning, salt, and pepper.

3. In a cast-iron pot with a heavy lid over medium-high heat, add the remaining 1 tablespoon (15 ml) oil. When sizzling, add the meat and brown on all sides, about 10 minutes. Add the onion, celery, rosemary, stock, and head of garlic and cover the pot.

4. Cook in the oven until the beef is fork tender, about 2 hours 30 minutes.

5. To serve, slice the meat and peel away any remaining membrane. Place on a platter with a spoonful of the gravy and vegetables poured over. Strain the remaining gravy into a separate bowl and thicken with cornstarch slurry if you like it thicker. Garnish with sprigs of fresh rosemary and serve with white rice.

FRANK FONTENOT MEAT MARKET

When I set out to find a beef tongue suitable for my black pot, my road led me to the Evangeline Parish town of Ville Platte, down a street flanking a railroad spur to a nondescript cinder block building. It didn't look like much, but what I found inside was a third-generation sausage maker and his wife turning out some of the most popular meat products in all of Acadiana.

The Frank Fontenot brand comes from a real man who was so proud of his trade that he put his name on the product. You see that a lot in these parts; it's kind of nice to know who made the food you are consuming. Frank started seventy years ago just after World War II in a makeshift sausage-making outpost in Prairie Ronde, Louisiana. His smoked sausage became widely sought, and he had the foresight to become USDA certified with a Louisiana State Department of Agriculture inspection sticker to be able to wholesale distribute his products throughout the region. Things took off.

Now Frank's grandson Jimmy and his wife Carylon carry on the family tradition of bringing quality Cajun smoked meats like andouille, tasso, pork sausage, turkey necks, ponce, and—of course—beef tongue to customers like me.

TATERS 'N ONIONS WITH COUNTRY HAM STEAK AND RED-EYE GRAVY

This dish is good most anytime—at supper in the evening or the next morning with a poached egg on top. The key is red-eye gravy—that rich, heady brew that seems to pump through the veins of most Southerners. It is praiseworthy indeed.

HAM STEAK AND RED-EYE GRAVY

1 large ½-inch (1.3 cm) thick, bone-in country ham steak, with fat ring trimmed and reserved

1 cup (240 ml) day-old dark roast coffee

1 tablespoon (12 g) dark brown sugar

1 teaspoon sugarcane molasses, such as Steen's (see Sources, page 232)

1 teaspoon freshly ground black pepper

TATERS 'N ONIONS

4 large russet potatoes

6 strips pork jowl bacon or smoked bacon

1 pound (455 g) bulk breakfast sausage with sage

8 ounces (227 g) diced tasso (see Sources, page 232) or smoked ham

2 large yellow onions, sliced

2 tablespoons (6 g) chopped fresh rosemary

1 teaspoon granulated sugar

Kosher salt and freshly ground black pepper

Dash of hot sauce

¼ cup (60 ml) chicken stock

4 poached eggs (optional)

HAM STEAK AND RED-EYE GRAVY

1. In a large cast-iron skillet over medium heat, add the trimmed fat from the ham. Cook until most of the fat is rendered out and then remove and discard the remaining pieces. Add the ham steak to the hot lard in the skillet and sear over medium-high heat until brown on one side, about 8 minutes. Turn and brown for 8 minutes on the other side, making sure to sear the outer surface of the ham steak until caramelized. Remove the ham steak to a platter and keep warm.

2. Turn the heat to high under the skillet and add the day-old coffee to the remaining fat and juices. Bring to a boil, add the brown sugar and cane molasses, and stir. Add the pepper and continue to cook for about 5 minutes until the liquid reduces to about ½ cup (120 ml) and takes on a syrupy consistency. Turn off the heat, pour the red-eye into a bowl, and keep at room temperature.

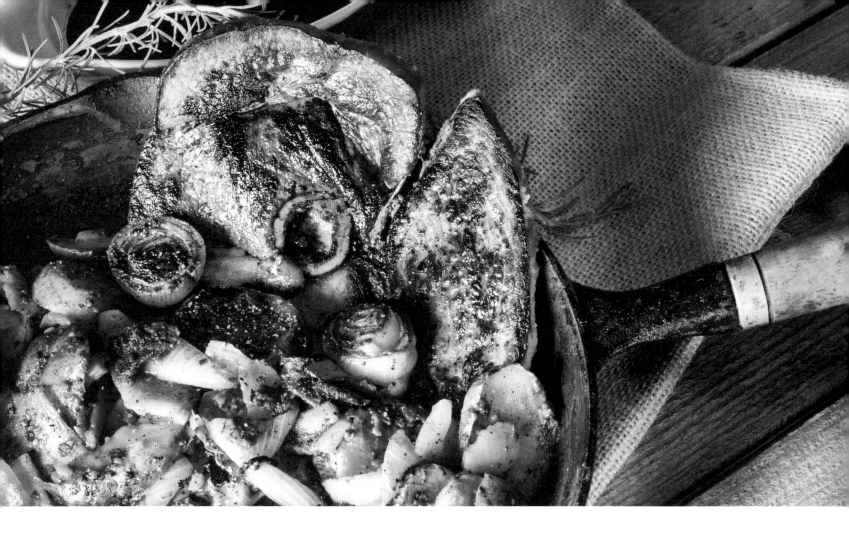

TATERS 'N ONIONS

1. Peel the potatoes and slice thinly into rounds. Set aside.

2. Wipe the bottom of the large cast-iron skillet from before and place over medium heat. Add the pork jowl bacon, fry for about 12 minutes or until crispy, and remove to a platter. Add the breakfast sausage to the leftover bacon grease and, using a spatula, break it down into small pieces. Stir for 8 minutes until browned and fully cooked. Remove to the platter with the bacon. Pour off most of the fat into a bowl and retain.

3. Add the tasso and sauté for about 5 minutes until slightly brown. Remove to the platter.

4. Add a few tablespoons (30 to 45 ml) of the reserved fat back to the skillet and turn the heat to medium-high. Add the sliced onions and cook until they begin to brown and start to caramelize, about 5 minutes. Add the chopped rosemary and stir to coat the onions. Remove to the platter with the meat.

5. Add a few tablespoons (30 to 45 ml) of the reserved fat back to the skillet and return the heat to medium-high.

Add the sliced potatoes and cook until they begin to brown and start to caramelize, about 5 minutes.

6. Lower the heat and return the onions, pork jowl bacon, sausage, and tasso to the pan and layer together, evenly distributing everything. Season the contents with the granulated sugar, salt, black pepper, and a dash of hot sauce. Once the skillet begins to sizzle, add the chicken stock and place the lid tightly on top. There should be very little steam escaping. Cook together for about 10 minutes. Remove the lid and continue cooking for 5 minutes or until most of the stock has evaporated. Once done, turn off the heat and cover until ready to serve.

7. Serve this dish family style by moving the black iron skillet to the center of the table. Place the ham steak on top and spoon some of the red-eye over the meat and let it drizzle into the potatoes and onions. Serve the rest of the gravy warm on the side.

8. If desired, add the poached eggs on top.

THE REVEREND'S RED-EYE

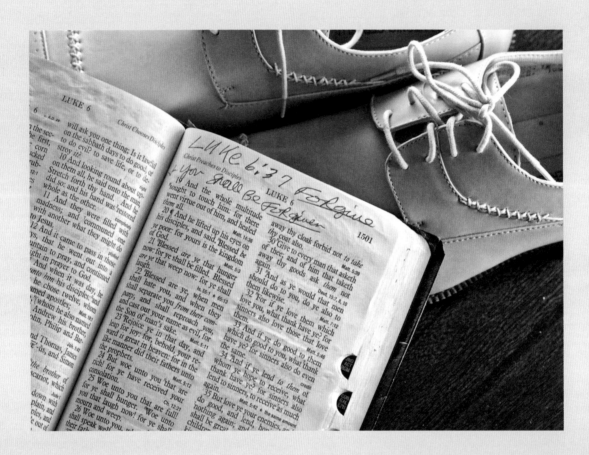

Reverend Jesse Waldrop is my wife's father and just plain Papaw to us. He's a transplanted Tennessee hillbilly preacher who found his way down to bayou country. For over forty years, the Reverend has walked the back roads of Acadiana spreading the gospel and selling the Good Book door-to-door. Known far and wide for his trademark blue shoes and his booming voice, he's a one-of-a-kind, bona fide original man of God.

According to Jesse, there are few things a man needs as along as he's got Jesus. But, if you were to ask him what he'd like to sit down to for his last supper before going to meet his maker, it'd be his family recipe of taters 'n onions along with a thick slab of country ham and red-eye.

I made my Taters 'n Onions with Country Ham Steak dish for the Reverend and embellished a bit on the Smoky Mountain version with a sweet and spicy, down-home, recipe. After a few bites, I waited for my judgment day. Papaw proclaimed it was "a good measure—pressed down, shaken together, and running over," and I guess Luke 6:38 is about as good as I could expect for my taters 'n onions, ham, and red-eye dinner.

You can judge for yourself.

SUNDAY GO-TO-EATIN'

In Cajun country, the most important meal of the week is Sunday dinner. Come to think of it, on most every other day of the week, the noonday meal is called "lunch," but when Sunday rolls around, it is always called "dinner"—a name that does justice to this time-honored family tradition. At least, that's the way it used to be.

Times change, and in the Graham family, as with many families, we wind up grabbing a quick bite after church, rushing off to watch the big game on TV, heading for the golf course, or whatever. It seems life moves faster these days; there's no longer time for traditions that once seemed so important. Well, I think it's high time to dial back the clock and return to those years of focused family life with time spent around the Sunday dinner table.

For the Graham family, the Sunday meal started after church and lasted all day long. It wasn't unusual to see a dozen or so taking part; uncles, aunts, and all the cousins would show up with casseroles and fixings to go along with the main course. While sweet tea was most often the drink of choice, freshly squeezed homemade lemonade often appeared on the table as well. The Sunday dinner was always served straight from the stovetop with big pots and foil trays lined up on the burners and along the kitchen counter.

Sunday dinner was a celebratory occasion to give thanks to God and family. The food was hearty; the helpings were large. Dirty rice, mashed potatoes, cabbage dressing, smothered green beans, boiled corn on the cob, baked beans, stewed black-eyes with ham hock, mustard potato salad, creamy coleslaw, and a huge tray of brown 'n serve rolls with a jar of fig preserves were always at the ready. It wasn't uncommon to see a variety of meats, but there was always—I mean always—a large pork roast taking center stage on the Sunday table.

REUNION TIME

The
Fontenot
Cuisine

D.F.

"1994"

CAJUN FRIED RICE WITH CRAWFISH AND GREEN ONION SAUSAGE

My mother-in-law, Rosalie Fontenot Waldrop, grew up in the Kings Farm community of Allen Parish, and she recalls her mother, Eve Fontenot, stirring a cast-iron skillet full of leftover rice and farm-fresh eggs into a simple farm-to-table breakfast dish. Not only is it a way to stretch a dollar, but it is a tasty, belly-filling meal for a hungry family. Serve with hot biscuits and Louisiana coffee (if you're serving this for breakfast).

1 cup (140 g) raw green onion pork sausage or raw Jimmy Dean–style breakfast sausage

1 cup (160 g) diced yellow onion

½ cup (60 g) diced celery

1 cup (180 g) chopped tomatoes

2 tablespoons (6 g) chopped fresh flat-leaf parsley

2 tablespoons (30 g) tomato paste

½ cup (120 ml) chicken stock, plus more if needed

4 cups (800 g) day-old cooked long-grain white rice (a bit dried out is best)

1 teaspoon paprika

Dash of hot sauce

Kosher salt and freshly ground black pepper

8 ounces (227 g) Louisiana crawfish tail meat (see Sources, page 232)

6 large eggs, divided

½ cup (50 g) diced green onion tops

1. Preheat the oven to 350°F (180°C).

2. In a cast-iron skillet over medium-high heat, add the sausage. Using a spatula, break the pieces into chunks and cook until brown, about 8 minutes. Remove to a platter.

3. In the same skillet, add the onion and celery to the remaining grease. Sauté until the onion turns translucent, about 5 minutes. Add the tomatoes and parsley, and cook for another 3 minutes. Add the tomato paste, stock, and rice. Stir to combine and season with the paprika, hot sauce, salt, and pepper.

4. Add the crawfish and chunks of sausage. In a small bowl, beat 2 of the eggs and add to the skillet. Gently stir the rice mixture to combine. Turn off the heat and, using a large spoon, make 4 indentations in the rice mixture. Crack the remaining 4 eggs into the indentations in the rice. Transfer the skillet to the oven and cook until the eggs begin to set and the rice is warmed through, about 10 minutes.

5. Top with the diced green onion and serve family style.

PORK ROAST WITH APPLE PAN GRAVY

When I think pork, I think apples. And when I think of the perfect Sunday dinner, my mind is already picturing my sweet and savory pork roast as the centerpiece for my table. With this recipe, I invite you to bring back Sunday dinner to your table and refocus on the importance of family and friends.

4 cups (960 ml) apple juice

1 cup (288 g) table salt

1 (6- to 8-pound [2.7 to 3.6 kg]) pork shoulder (Boston butt) roast, bone in

2 cups (300 g) ice

2 tablespoons (30 ml) vegetable oil

2 tablespoons (16 g) Sweet Heat Seasoning (page 231)

6 cloves garlic

1 cup (160 g) chopped yellow onion

1 cup (150 g) chopped green bell pepper

1 cup (240 ml) apple cider

1 cup (240 g) applesauce

2 cups (480 ml) chicken stock

4 medium apples, 2 cored and sliced, 2 left whole

¼ cup (15 g) chopped flat-leaf parsley

2 sprigs fresh rosemary

1 tablespoon (15 g) butter

Kosher salt and freshly ground black pepper

1. In a large container with a lid, pour in the apple juice and salt and stir to combine. Add the pork and ice. Cover the container and refrigerate for 8 hours or overnight. Remove the pork roast and pat dry.

2. Preheat the oven to 300°F (150°C).

3. Rub the roast with the oil and sprinkle with the Sweet Heat Seasoning. Make 1-inch (2.5 cm) slits in the roast and insert the garlic cloves.

4. In a large cast-iron pot or Dutch oven with a tight-fitting lid over medium-high heat, add the roast. Brown on all sides, including the fat cap, about 12 minutes. Add the onion and bell pepper and cook until the onion turns translucent, about 5 minutes. Pour in the apple cider to deglaze the pan. Add the applesauce, stock, sliced apples, whole apples, parsley, and rosemary to the pot. Place the roast fat-side-up on top of the vegetables; cover and roast for 2 hours. Uncover and roast for 1 hour longer until the fat cap browns and the meat reaches an internal temperature of 170°F (77°C) on a meat thermometer, or until fork tender. Remove the pork roast from the pot and place on a platter to rest, covered with foil.

5. Place the pot with the pan juices and drippings on the stovetop. Remove the rosemary stems. Turn the heat to high, bring the mixture to a boil, and reduce to a simmer. Add the butter at the end and stir to incorporate. Taste the gravy and season with salt and pepper, if needed.

6. Slice the roast (it should begin to fall apart) and remove the shoulder bone. Serve on a platter with all of the pan drippings and pieces of apple along with the gravy on the side.

SERVES 4

PREP TIME: 30 MINUTES
COOK TIME: 2 HOURS 30 MINUTES
TOTAL TIME: 3 HOURS

SOUP BONE OSSO BUCO

When I see osso buco—the Italian wine-braised meat specialty—on a menu, I almost always order it. So when my wife decided to make a pot of vegetable soup and came home from the grocery store with a bag full of fresh vegetables, tomatoes, stock, and a pack of inexpensive beef shank soup bones, a culinary light bulb went off. Yeah, a tasty full-flavored osso buco at half the cost. Why not? Serve over mashed potatoes or white rice.

4 (10-ounce [280 g]) cross-cut beef shanks with marrowbone

Kosher salt and freshly ground black pepper

½ cup (60 g) unbleached all-purpose flour

2 tablespoons (30 ml) vegetable oil

2 cups (480 ml) dry red wine

2 cups (480 ml) beef stock

1 cup (160 g) diced yellow onion

1 cup (120 g) diced celery

½ cup (60 g) chopped fennel bulb (omit if you don't like the flavor)

1 large ripe tomato, roughly chopped

1 (10-ounce [280 g]) can mild diced tomatoes and green chiles, drained

1 tablespoon (8 g) minced garlic

1 tablespoon (3 g) chopped fresh sage leaves

1 tablespoon (3 g) chopped fresh rosemary

½ cup (25 g) chopped flat-leaf parsley

2 bay leaves

1 teaspoon Cajun Seasoning Blend (page 231)

1. Season the beef shanks with salt and pepper, and coat all sides with the flour.

2. In a cast-iron pot or skillet with a heavy lid over medium-high heat, add the oil. Place the meat in the oil and brown both sides, about 8 minutes. Pour off any excess oil and add the wine to deglaze the pot. Let the wine cook off for 3 minutes and then add the stock.

3. Lower the heat to a simmer and add the onion, celery, fennel (if using), tomato, canned tomatoes, garlic, sage, rosemary, parsley, bay leaves, Cajun seasoning, and a pinch of salt and pepper. Cover and let simmer for 2 hours. Remove the bay leaves.

4. Uncover and check to see that the meat is fork tender. Taste the gravy, and season with salt and pepper if needed.

SHRIMP AND MIRLITON POT PIE

Every tasty recipe is a road map to a new and undiscovered place. This unique combination of down-home Southern ingredients is well worth the trip. Just think of it: briny shrimp and farm-fresh vegetables cooked down in a thick, creamy filling and topped with a crispy golden brown crust.

This recipe takes a couple of back road shortcuts with the addition of cream of shrimp soup and store-bought piecrust. It's a convenient detour to arrive at a most tasty destination. So, let's go off-the-eatin' path, and discover delicious new tastes with this creative take on a Southern classic.

1 tablespoon (15 g) unsalted butter

1 tablespoon (15 ml) olive oil

1 pound (455 g) medium (41/50 count) shrimp, peeled and deveined

1 tablespoon (8 g) smoked paprika

2 cups (320 g) diced yellow onion

1 cup (120 g) diced celery

½ cup (75 g) chopped multicolor sweet bell pepper

1 cup (120 g) sliced carrot

1 medium mirliton, seeded and diced into ¼-inch (6 mm) cubes

2 medium red potatoes, diced into ¼-inch (6 mm) cubes (peeled if desired)

1 tablespoon (8 g) minced garlic

2 tablespoons (6 g) chopped fresh flat-leaf parsley

1 tablespoon (3 g) chopped fresh rosemary

1 teaspoon chopped fresh basil

2 tablespoons (16 g) all-purpose flour

1 (10.5-ounce [294 g]) can cream of shrimp soup, such as Campbell's

1 cup (240 ml) chicken stock, plus more if needed

1 teaspoon Cajun Seasoning Blend (page 231)

Kosher salt and freshly ground black pepper

1 cup (150 g) frozen green peas

1 (10-inch [25 cm]) frozen, ready-made, deep-dish piecrust, thawed

1 large egg, beaten

2 tablespoons (10 g) grated Parmesan cheese

1. In a large ovenproof nonstick skillet over medium-high heat, add the butter and olive oil. With paper towels, pat the shrimp dry, and once the pan is sizzling hot, add the shrimp and evenly sprinkle with the paprika. Sauté just until the shrimp turn pink on both sides, about 5 minutes. Remove the shrimp to a platter and keep warm.

2. In the remaining butter and olive oil in the same large nonstick skillet over medium-high heat, add the onion, celery, bell pepper, and carrot. Cook until the onion turns translucent, about 5 minutes. Add the mirliton, potatoes, garlic, parsley, rosemary, and basil. Lower the heat and continue cooking for another 5 minutes.

3. Add the flour, sprinkling it evenly around the skillet. Stir the flour into the vegetables and cook for 5 minutes, or until the raw flour taste is gone.

4. Add the soup and chicken stock and stir to combine. Season with the Cajun seasoning, salt, and pepper. Continue cooking the mixture at a simmer until the mirliton and potatoes are tender, about 10 minutes. Be sure to add more stock if the mixture becomes too thick.

5. Add the green peas and shrimp and stir the mixture to incorporate. You want a moist and ultra-thick pie-like texture for the filling—not soupy. Turn off the heat and let the pan cool or refrigerate until ready to bake the pot pie.

6. Preheat the oven to 400°F (200°C).

7. Roll out the piecrust and use your cooking vessel to measure the diameter of the desired circle; leave extra dough around the edge to seal. Cut holes in the middle to vent steam. Place the piecrust over the skillet containing the shrimp and vegetable mixture. Fold and crimp the edges to seal. Add a bit of water to the beaten egg and whisk. Using a pastry brush, lightly brush the top and edges of the crust with the egg wash. Sprinkle with the Parmesan cheese.

8. Transfer the skillet to the oven and bake until the crust is golden brown, about 30 minutes. Remove the pot pie from the oven and let rest for 5 minutes before serving.

BUTTERNUT AND SHRIMP PASTA

Fresh squash, pumpkin, and gourds of all kinds begin showing up at the local farmers' markets in autumn. It always puts me in the mood for a delicious recipe featuring those flavors, and with this shrimp and pasta dish, I can't think of a better way to usher in the fall season.

2 tablespoons (36 g) table salt

1 bunch (approximately 10 spears) asparagus, chopped into large pieces

1 pound (455 g) pappardelle pasta

1 tablespoon (15 ml) olive oil

1 yellow onion, chopped

1 cup (120 g) chopped celery

1 cup (120 g) chopped carrot

1 cup (150 g) chopped sweet bell pepper

1 tablespoon (8 g) minced garlic

4 cups (960 ml) butternut squash soup, such as Imagine® Organic Creamy Butternut Squash Soup

1 cup (240 ml) heavy cream

1 tablespoon (8 g) Cajun Seasoning Blend (page 231)

1 cup (100 g) diced green onion tops

2 tablespoons (6 g) chopped flat-leaf parsley, plus more for garnish

Kosher salt and freshly ground black pepper

1 pound (455 g) jumbo (16/20 count) shrimp, shells removed, tails on or off

1. Fill a large pot halfway with water, add the table salt, and bring to a boil over high heat. Add the asparagus and cook until just blanched but still crunchy, about 1 minute. Remove the asparagus and add to a bowl of ice water to stop the cooking and preserve the color. Add the pasta noodles to the water and cook until al dente. Drain the noodles, reserving 1 cup (240 ml) of the pasta water for later use.

2. In a large pot over medium-high heat, add the olive oil. When it's hot, add the onion, celery, carrot, and bell pepper. Sauté until the onion turns translucent, about 5 minutes. Add the garlic and cook for another 2 minutes. Add the butternut squash soup and cream and stir to combine. When it begins to bubble, lower the heat to a simmer and cook until the mixture reduces and thickens, about 5 minutes.

3. Add the Cajun seasoning, green onion, and parsley and stir to combine. Taste the mixture and season to taste with kosher salt and pepper. Add enough pasta to the sauce to accommodate the number of guests you are serving (Note: Save any leftover pasta to add back to the sauce later.) Turn off the heat and let the pasta soak in the hot sauce for another 5 minutes.

4. Heat the pot containing the pasta and sauce and add the shrimp and the parboiled asparagus. Cook until the shrimp turn pink and cook through, about 5 minutes. If the sauce becomes too thick, add some of the reserved pasta water to thin it out to a sauce consistency (thick enough to coat the back of a spoon). Serve in bowls and garnish with a sprig of parsley.

RABBIT AND DUMPLINGS

I love the way these pillowy, soft dumplings sink into a bed of herb-infused rabbit meat and soak up the spicy blanket of gravy for what I can only describe as comfort food.

DUMPLINGS

2½ cups (300 g) unbleached all-purpose flour

½ cup (110 g) non-fat dry, powdered milk

¼ cup (55 g) baking powder

1 teaspoon sugar

1 teaspoon salt

½ cup (120 ml) canola oil

1 cup (240 ml) whole milk, plus more if needed

RABBIT

1 (2.5 pound [1.2 kg]) whole rabbit

Kosher salt and freshly ground black pepper

¼ cup (60 ml) vegetable oil

2 cups (320 g) roughly chopped yellow onion

1 cup (120 g) roughly chopped celery

1 cup (150 g) roughly chopped green bell pepper

1 cup (120 g) sliced carrots

1 tablespoon (8 g) minced garlic

2 tablespoons (6 g) chopped flat-leaf parsley

1 sprig rosemary

1 teaspoon chopped thyme

8 cups (1.9L) dark chicken stock, plus more if needed

DUMPLINGS

1. In a large mixing bowl, add the flour, dry milk, baking powder, sugar, and salt. Mix together. While whisking, slowly drizzle in the canola oil. Continue whisking until the mix becomes wet with a meal-like texture. If you like, this mix can now be covered, refrigerated, and held until ready to make the dumpling batter.

2. To make the batter, whisk half of the milk into the mix until thoroughly combined. Continue adding milk until the mixture becomes wet and very thick but not runny like pancake batter. Cover and refrigerate until ready to use.

RABBIT

1. Cut the rabbit into quarters and then cut the back in half. Season with salt and pepper.

2. Unpackage the organ meats, if using. Rinse them in cold water and reserve.

3. In a large cast-iron pot over medium-high heat, add 2 tablespoons (30 ml) of oil. Once the oil is smoking, add the rabbit skin-side down. Brown the rabbit on all sides and remove to a platter.

4. Add the onion, celery, bell pepper, and carrots, along with the remaining oil, if needed. Cook until the onion turns translucent, about 5 minutes. Add the garlic, parsley, rosemary, and thyme. Continue cooking for another 3 minutes.

5. Meanwhile, in another pan over high heat, add the chicken stock and all the rabbit organ meats, if using. Bring to a boil and then lower the heat to simmer for 5 minutes. Remove the organ meats and chop into very small pieces. Add the organ meats to the pot with the vegetables.

6. Add the rabbit pieces to the pot and pour over the chicken stock. Cover and let cook on the stovetop at a simmer for 1 hour.

7. Check to see that the rabbit is fork-tender and there is still sufficient liquid in the pot. If not, add additional stock. Turn off the heat until ready to add the dumplings to finish the dish.

8. Bring the pot containing the rabbit and stock to a boil. Lower the heat to a simmer. Using a large spoon, scoop a 1-tablespoon-size portion of the dumpling mix. Drop the dumplings into the stock around the rabbit pieces. Place them so that they are not touching. Let simmer uncovered on the stovetop for 10 minutes. Cover and cook for another 10 minutes. Turn off the heat, but leave the pot covered. Serve immediately.

NOTES While you can cook the rabbit and vegetables in advance and hold, once the dumplings are added you should serve this dish immediately while they are light and fluffy. Waiting or cooking ahead will allow the dumplings to become dense and tough. I do not recommend reheating the leftover dumplings the following day.

MACADAMIA NUT ICE CREAM SANDWICHES

The rich sweetened cream contrasts with the saltiness of roasted macadamia nuts, and when combined between two cookies, my Macadamia Nut Ice Cream Sandwich is a study in the art of sandwich making—ice cream style.

ICE CREAM

1½ cups (360 ml) sweetened condensed milk

1 cup (240 ml) unsweetened macadamia nut milk or whole milk

1 teaspoon vanilla extract

2 cups (480 ml) heavy whipping cream

1 cup (140 g) roasted macadamia nuts, roughly chopped

COOKIES AND ASSEMBLY

2½ cups (300 g) all-purpose flour

1 teaspoon baking soda

Pinch of salt

1 cup (240 g) salted butter, at room temperature

½ cup (120 g) light brown sugar

2 eggs

1 tablespoon (15 ml) vanilla extract

3 cups (420 g) roasted macadamia nuts, roughly chopped into large pieces, divided

ICE CREAM

1. In a large mixing bowl, add the condensed milk, macadamia nut milk, and vanilla. Whisk to combine.

2. With an electric hand mixer in another bowl, beat the cream until it forms stiff peaks. Fold the whipped cream into the milk mixture and fold in the chopped macadamia nuts, distributing evenly.

3. Pour the mixture into a covered container and freeze overnight.

COOKIES AND ASSEMBLY

1. In a large mixing bowl, add the flour, baking soda, and salt. Stir to combine.

2. In another bowl, add the butter and brown sugar and stir to combine. Add the eggs and vanilla, and stir to combine.

3. Add the wet ingredients to the dry and stir in 1 cup (140 g) of the nuts. Cover and refrigerate until the dough is chilled, about 45 minutes.

4. Preheat the oven to 350°F (180°C). Grease a baking sheet.

5. Using a standard ice cream scoop, portion out the dough onto the prepared baking sheet. Separate the balls of dough so that they will have room to spread out and bake evenly. (The size of your dough ball will determine the size of your ice cream sandwich, so adjust accordingly.)

6. Bake until crispy golden brown, 10 to 15 minutes. Cool for 1 hour until the cookies have hardened before making the ice cream sandwiches.

7. To assemble, take the ice cream out of the freezer and let sit for 20 minutes. Pour out the remaining 2 cups (280 g) chopped nuts onto a cutting board.

8. Place a cookie on the cutting board and add a heaping scoop of ice cream to

SERVES 4

PREP TIME: 1 HOUR
COOK TIME: 15 MINUTES
TOTAL TIME: 1 HOUR 15 MINUTES

the center. Place another cookie on top and gently press down until the ice cream spreads out to the edges. Place the ice cream edge of the sandwich into the chopped nuts and rotate until coated all around. Place on a tray and freeze immediately. Repeat with all the ice cream sandwiches.

NOTES You determine the size of your ice cream sandwich by the size of your cookie. Be sure to bake the cookies until they harden (not a soft gooey texture) so that the "sandwich" will hold together.

SWEET MEMORIES

Back when I was a kid, every neighborhood had its corner grocery. You know the kind I mean: the nice lady with the big smile behind the counter, the crotchety owner who shooed you away when you lingered too long, and an endless variety of sweet treats that made that pocket full of change a treasure chest. My store was the Corner Cash.

The shop was just a short bike ride from my house, and I always leaned my Schwinn against the pine tree just outside; it was my reserved parking spot. I can still hear the screeching of that taut spring-loaded screen door open and slam shut behind me. It always startled me. Even at ten years old, the wood floors creaked as I walked straight to the reach-in freezer for my obsession—an ice cream sandwich.

These weren't your typical ice cream sandwiches; these were Red Bird ice cream sandwiches. A two-inch-thick square of vanilla ice cream encased in a chocolate brownie-like cookie crust with a cardboard band wrapped around the middle. I was an expert at busting open the paper wrapper, discarding that center band, and taking that first bite, all within seconds of plunking down my quarter. It was glorious.

The Red Bird Ice Cream Company, owned by the Cutrer family, sold their products everywhere and were revered by a loyal regional following. Ice cream and sherbet were their focus and they distributed to restaurants, retail, and even to local schools. But of all their products, that ice cream sandwich had a grip on me. My daddy's restaurant sold them, and he stocked the reach-in freezer on our screened-in back porch with them. Needless to say, I had lots of friends.

Like the old Corner Cash, the Red Bird has long since disappeared. And although I've never tasted an ice cream sandwich that rivals that one, I've learned to make my own following a few basic rules. It might not be the ice cream sandwich of my youth, but for the ten-year-old boy that still lives within me, it is sweet comfort indeed.

SWEET POTATO SHAKE

While you don't normally think of the fall as a time to bring out the milkshake mixer, it's hard not to fall in love with the idea of a creamy, dreamy sweet potato shake with all the flavors of the holidays mixed up in an ice-cold glass. It's time to shake up the season.

2 large sweet potatoes, baked, or 2 cups (480 g) canned sweet potato puree

2 teaspoons ground cinnamon, divided, plus more for garnish

2 teaspoons light brown sugar, divided

1 large raw sweet potato

1 (½-gallon [2 L]) carton vanilla ice cream

1 cup (240 ml) whole milk

1. Slice open the baked sweet potatoes, scoop out the flesh, eliminating any stringy membranes, and transfer the potato to a mixing bowl. Add 1 teaspoon each of the cinnamon and light brown sugar. With a wire whisk, beat the potato until completely smooth. Chill in the refrigerator for at least 1 hour or until time to serve.

2. Cut 4 round slices of raw sweet potato and place in a microwavable container with a few tablespoons (30 to 45 ml) of water. Cover the container and microwave on high until the potato rounds steam and become tender, about 5 minutes. Remove the potato rounds from the container and pat dry. Sprinkle both sides of the rounds with the remaining 1 teaspoon cinnamon and remaining 1 teaspoon brown sugar.

3. For each shake, start by adding 2 generous scoops of ice cream to the metal mixing container of a milkshake machine or the container of a blender. Add 2 heaping tablespoons (30 g) of sweet potato pulp and a splash of milk. On high speed, mix the ingredients, adding more ice cream or milk if needed to create a thick shake. Pour the mixture into a tall glass and dust the top of the creamy shake with a sprinkle of cinnamon. Garnish with a sweet potato round and serve with both a spoon and straw.

NOTES Prep time does not include baking the sweet potatoes. Substitute other fall flavors like pumpkin in this recipe for a taste of the season.

PREP TIME: 1 HOUR
COOK TIME: 1 HOUR
TOTAL TIME: 2 HOURS

PRALINE PUMPKIN PIE

There is no other farm-to-table ingredient that defines a season more than pumpkin, and here in Louisiana we have an endless list of sweet and savory recipes to use them. This praline pumpkin pie is a slice of the season with the pungent flavors of cinnamon, allspice, nutmeg, and ginger wafting through the house. With the crunch of Louisiana pecans and the punch of praline liqueur, this is a pumpkin pie to write about. Serve with a dollop of whipped cream and a drizzle of praline liqueur on top.

PRALINE TOPPING AND CRUST

¼ cup (50 g) plus 1 tablespoon (12 g) granulated sugar, divided

2 tablespoons (30 g) dark brown sugar

⅛ teaspoon ground ginger

⅛ teaspoon ground nutmeg

⅛ teaspoon ground cinnamon

¾ cup (90 g) all-purpose flour, plus more for rolling

1 tablespoon (15 ml) praline liqueur (see Sources, page 232)

4 tablespoons (60 g) cold unsalted butter, cut into chunks

¾ cup (105 g) roughly chopped pecans

2 (10-inch [25 cm]) store-bought rolled piecrusts (not in the tin)

1 egg, beaten

PRALINE TOPPING AND CRUST

1. In a stainless steel mixing bowl, add ¼ cup (50 g) of the granulated sugar, brown sugar, spices, and flour. Blend and add the praline liqueur and the cold butter in chunks. With your fingers or a pastry blender, incorporate the butter into the dry ingredients until it becomes crumbly in texture. Add the pecans and evenly distribute throughout the mixture. Refrigerate until ready to use. (This is important so the butter chills.)

2. Dust the counter with flour and place the two piecrusts on top. Position one on top of the other and begin rolling until they come together and spread out to a 14-inch (35.5 cm)-diameter circle.

3. In a 10-inch (25 cm) black iron skillet coated with nonstick spray, add the crust and position it to fill the interior of the pan. Tuck the edges of the crust around the skillet in a rough and rustic manner. Brush the edges of the dough with the beaten egg and sprinkle with the remaining 1 tablespoon (12 g) granulated sugar. Refrigerate until ready to use.

PUMPKIN PIE FILLING

1. Preheat the oven to 350°F (180°C).

2. In a large mixing bowl, add the pumpkin, brown sugar, milk, spices, molasses, liqueur, and salt. Whisk together until blended. Add the eggs and the yolk and whisk until fully incorporated.

3. Pour the filling into the piecrust and smooth out the pie.

4. Add the streusel topping to the top, being careful to evenly distribute the pecans.

5. Bake on the center rack until the pie filling sets (test with a skewer) and the crust is golden brown, 45 minutes to 1 hour.

6. Remove from the oven, let cool, and then chill in the refrigerator for at least 4 hours. Serve cold or at room temperature.

PUMPKIN PIE FILLING

1 (29-ounce [812 g]) can pumpkin, such as Libby's Pure Pumpkin

½ cup (120 g) dark brown sugar

½ cup (120 ml) canned evaporated milk

¼ teaspoon ground ginger

¼ teaspoon ground nutmeg

¼ teaspoon ground allspice

¼ teaspoon ground ginger

¼ teaspoon ground cinnamon

1 tablespoon (18 g) sugarcane molasses, such as Steen's (see Sources, page 232)

2 tablespoons (30 ml) praline liqueur or almond- or pecan-flavored liqueur

Pinch of salt

3 large eggs plus 1 egg yolk

NOTES For skillet pies like this, I've found that packaged piecrusts tend to be too small, so I double them up and roll them out for a crustier pie dough.

LO'S APPLE PIE

Just ask my daughter what her favorite dessert is, and you'll get a resounding answer: pie. Pie of most any kind will do, but when it comes to getting in the kitchen and making a pie from scratch, Lo goes apple all the way.

When my daughter Lauren (Lo) was just counter height, Roxanne and I recall baking pies with her. She loved getting her hands in the dough and flour in her hair while making apple pie. And for us, we were making memories—warm family moments filled with love and laughter, with just a hint of cinnamon. And now, whenever she returns home, we make Lo's Apple Pie once again.

With its unstructured piecrust baked in a cast-iron skillet, this pie comes out of the oven taking on the role of an American classic with all the charm of a deep-dish Louisiana skillet pie. Looking at this rough-edged and rustic outer crust baked to a golden brown, you will be torn between taking photos or taking a bite. Lo's apple pie is hard to resist, and with its free-form, store-bought crust, it is easy.

6 sweet apples, such as Honeycrisp

¾ cup (150 g) sugar, plus more for sprinkling

2 tablespoons (16 g) all-purpose flour, plus more for rolling

¾ teaspoon ground cinnamon

¼ teaspoon salt

⅛ teaspoon ground nutmeg

1 tablespoon (15 ml) freshly squeezed lemon juice

2 (9-inch [23 cm]) store-bought piecrusts, 1 in the tin and 1 rolled

1 egg, beaten

1. Preheat the oven to 425°F (220°C). Coat the inside of a 9-inch (23 cm) cast-iron skillet with nonstick spray. Line a baking sheet with parchment paper.

2. Core the apples, chop into ¼-inch (6 mm) cubes, and add to a large mixing bowl along with the sugar and flour. Add the cinnamon, salt, nutmeg, and lemon juice, and combine to coat the apples evenly.

3. Remove the piecrust from the tin and place in the prepared skillet. Pour the apple filling into the crust and mound in the center.

4. Sprinkle the counter with extra flour, and roll out the second piecrust until it measures 10 inches (25 cm) in diameter. Add the piecrust over the top of the filling and fold in the edges. Cut four vents in the top of the crust, brush with the egg wash, and sprinkle with extra sugar. If you like, cut decorative shapes (we like leaves) out of the leftover pie dough and place on top.

5. Place the skillet on the prepared baking sheet and place in the center of the oven. Bake for 40 minutes or until golden brown. Remove and let the pie cool until ready to serve.

NOTES This is not your typical mushy apple pie filling but rather an unstructured one that renders the apples cooked but still crisp. Add another tablespoon of flour if you want your filling firmer.

CHAPTER 4

WINTER

IT IS MY GOAL TO DIG DEEP AND GET TO THE ROOTS

of Louisiana cooking. Plain and simple, backbone stew made the traditional French Acadian way is an induction into the inner circle of rural Cajun cooking. You won't see this Cajun recipe on mainstream menus, and aside from an occasional steam table lunchroom, this dish is relegated to home stovetops and backyard propane cookers.

To discover the art of a rural Cajun backbone stew, I took a trek to Eunice, Louisiana, on a frosty winter morning for a Cajun *boucherie* (pig roast). Pulling up to the fairgrounds on the outskirts of the small St. Landry Parish town, I was led across a field to a cluster of spreading oaks and a crew of two dozen men and women already hard at work. The 160-pound (73 kg) hog was spread out on a large wooden table and scalding hot water was poured over to loosen the skin so the hair could easily be scraped away.

Torches, butcher knives, and saws were busy burning, slicing, and dissecting the hair, skin, and meat of the pig. Chopping boards spread out across long tables, and folks were busy tending to a dozen or so cast-iron and Magnalite pots. Smokers, meat grinders, and sausage stuffers were prepped and ready to receive their cuts, and charcoal grills were fired up with embers aglow. These artisans of French Acadian heritage clearly knew their task at hand, and each was an expert in their specialty Cajun recipe.

The hog's head was severed and moved off for head cheese-making, and the pig's feet were cut

above the shank and blowtorched to remove any remaining hair. The liver was used for boudin, the stomach for a recipe called ponce, and the organ meats for fraisseurs (butcher's stew). The ribs were destined for the grill, and the backbone—the prize cut—was reserved for the stew pot. A propane burner blasted away as pork stock infused with dark roux boiled gently in an enormous black iron caldron. The Cajun trinity of chopped vegetables—onion, celery, and bell pepper—soon joined the bony chunks of meat in the backbone stew pot. A heavy dose of cayenne and garlic spiced the brew, and a low and slow simmer produced the magic.

Backbone stew is the underbelly of Cajun black pot cooking. A complex, darkly divine stew of pork backbone floating in a bowl of roux-infused and pig's feet-thickened gravy, this is a dish so regally rich, so potently porky, so decadently deep in flavor that you might never come up for air.

BACKBONE STEW

Now, don't be intimidated: this Cajun recipe can easily be made in your home kitchen no matter where you live. It might take a search for some out-of-the-norm ingredients (ask your butcher for pork backbone and feet), but truth be told, much of Louisiana cooking uses familiar ingredients, many of which are easily sourced. Serve with hot French bread.

8 strips smoked bacon, chopped

2 cups (320 g) diced yellow onion

2 cups (240 g) diced celery

2 cups (300 g) chopped green bell pepper

1 cup (50 g) chopped flat-leaf parsley

1 tablespoon (8 g) minced garlic

8 cups (1.9 L) pork (preferably) or chicken stock, plus more if needed

1 cup (240 ml) Dark Cajun Roux (page 230), plus more if needed

5 pounds (1.8 kg) pork backbone with meat attached, cut into 4-inch (10 cm) chunks

2 tablespoons (16 g) Cajun Seasoning Blend (page 231)

2 pig's feet

Kosher salt and freshly ground black pepper

Dash of hot sauce

6 cups (1.2 kg) cooked long-grain white rice

2 cups (200 g) diced green onion tops, for serving

1. In a large cast-iron pot with a heavy lid over medium-high heat, add the bacon and cook until crispy, about 8 minutes. Remove the bacon for later use. Remove all but 2 tablespoons (30 ml) of the remaining bacon grease.

2. In the same pot over medium-high heat, add the onion, celery, and bell pepper to the remaining bacon grease. Cook until the vegetables are browned, about 8 minutes, and then add the parsley and garlic and stir to combine. Add the stock and roux, and bring to a boil. Lower the heat to a simmer.

3. Sprinkle the pork backbone pieces with the Cajun seasoning, and add to the pot along with the pig's feet and cooked bacon pieces. Cover and simmer for 1 hour.

4. Check to see that the stew is thickening and, if needed, add more roux. If it is too thick, add a bit more stock. Season to taste with salt and pepper. Cover and cook for another 1 hour 30 minutes.

5. Uncover and check to see that the meat from the backbone is fork tender and turn off the heat. Taste the gravy and add hot sauce to taste.

6. Remove the pig's feet from the pot and pick the meat from the bones, discarding the skin, bones, and cartilage. Add the picked meat back to the pot.

7. Serve a couple of the backbone pieces over white rice in a bowl with plenty of gravy. Garnish with a sprinkle of green onion.

NOTES Have your butcher reserve the backbone that is cut away from the pork loin during butchering. Pork neck bones can also be used. I like using a flavored (pork, preferably) stock for this, but many old-school Cajun cooks will use water. You might think the pig's feet are optional, but I urge you to add them. The velvet texture and natural thickening of the gravy will astound you. Most any good butcher can stock you up with cleaned pig's feet or you can find them at an Asian grocery.

RAGIN' CAJUN RED BEAN CHILI

First, the idea: turn a pot of creamy down-home Louisiana red beans spiked with Ragin' Cajuns beer and Latin spices into a meaty porkalicious chili. This unique recipe solves the debate on whether to add beans to your chili: the beans are the star of this bowl o' red. Serve with ice-cold beer and crackers.

1 (16-ounce [455 g]) package dried red kidney beans (do not use canned)

2 tablespoons (30 ml) bacon grease or vegetable oil, divided

1 cup (160 g) diced yellow onion

1 cup (160 g) diced red onion

1 cup (120 g) diced celery

2 tablespoons (16 g) minced garlic

1 tablespoon (8 g) diced fresh jalapeño pepper, seeds and ribs removed

2 (12-ounce [360 ml]) bottles full-bodied beer, such as Ragin' Cajuns ale (see Sources, page 232)

2 cups (480 ml) water, plus more as needed

1 pound (455 g) ground pork

1 tablespoon (8 g) all-purpose flour

1 tablespoon (8 g) Cajun Seasoning Blend (page 231)

1 tablespoon (8 g) chili powder

1 teaspoon ground cumin

1 (10-ounce [280 g]) can mild diced tomatoes with green chiles, drained

2 cups (480 ml) tomato puree

1 tablespoon (15 g) tomato paste

1 tablespoon (8 g) finely chopped canned chipotle peppers in adobo sauce with 1 tablespoon (15 ml) sauce

Kosher salt and freshly ground black pepper

2 tablespoons (2 g) chopped fresh cilantro

6 cups (1.2 kg) cooked long-grain white rice

1 cup (100 g) diced green onion tops

1. Soak the beans overnight by placing the red beans into a container and covering them with water. The next morning, drain the beans and reserve.

2. In a black iron pot with a heavy lid over medium-high heat, add 1 tablespoon (15 ml) of the bacon grease. When hot, add the onions, celery, garlic, and jalapeño; cook until the onions turn translucent, about 5 minutes.

3. Add the drained red beans, beer, and 2 cups (480 ml) water to cover. Bring to a boil over high heat. Decrease the heat to a simmer and cover the pot. Cook for 1 hour or until the beans are tender. Pour the beans and all the liquid into a container and reserve.

4. Wipe the pot clean and place over medium-high heat. Add the remaining 1 tablespoon (15 ml) bacon grease; when hot, add the pork and sauté, breaking up the meat into chunks with the back of your spoon, until browned, about 8 minutes. Sprinkle the flour over the meat and drippings in the pot and continue stirring until the raw flour taste cooks out, about 5 minutes.

5. Add the beans and all the liquid to the pot along with the Cajun seasoning, chili powder, cumin, diced tomatoes with green chiles, tomato puree, tomato paste, and chipotle with adobo sauce. Bring to a simmer, cover, and cook for 30 minutes.

6. Uncover and stir. Check the level of the liquid and add more water so that the liquid comes above the top of the beans; cover the pot and cook for another 30 minutes.

BAYOU TECHE BREWING

My friend Karlos Knott, brewmaster at Bayou Teche Brewing in Arnaudville, Louisiana, brews Ragin' Cajuns ale (see Sources, page 232). Named for the University of Louisiana Lafayette Ragin' Cajuns football team, this is the first officially licensed college beer. This German-style ale is made with Louisiana rice, barley, and hops for a balanced taste that works perfectly in this pot of Ragin' Cajun Red Bean Chili.

7. Uncover and taste to see that the beans have absorbed the spices and are fully cooked. Season with salt and pepper and add the chopped cilantro. Cover the pot and continue to simmer over very low heat for 30 minutes. Remove the pot from the stovetop and place on a large cutting board for serving family style.

8. A traditional rural Cajun way of eating chili, especially red bean chili, is to serve it over white rice. Ladle the chili over rice into bowls and garnish with a sprinkle of diced green onion.

SMOKED WINGS

These wings take flight in a combination of Korean and Louisiana Spices with a dark and smoky taste that blends the best of both cultures. If you're tired of the same ol' chicken wing recipe, then read on and discover this flavor-filled combination.

3 cups (720 ml) buttermilk

½ cup (144 g) salt

2 tablespoons (16 g) Cajun Seasoning Blend (page 231)

40 chicken wings

¼ cup (30 g) Sweet Heat Seasoning (page 231)

¼ cup (60 ml) soy sauce

¼ cup (60 ml) Worcestershire sauce

¼ cup (85 g) sugarcane molasses, such as Steen's (see Sources, page 232)

2 tablespoons (30 ml) sriracha sauce

2 tablespoons (30 ml) sesame oil

2 tablespoons (16 g) ground ginger

2 tablespoons (16 g) chili powder

2 tablespoons (16 g) minced garlic

2 tablespoons (18 g) white sesame seeds

1 cup (100 g) sliced green onion tops

4 cups (800 g) cooked brown rice

1. For the brine, add the buttermilk, salt, and Cajun seasoning to a large container with a tight-fitting lid. Add the wings and stir to combine. Add water to the brine if more liquid is needed to cover the wings. Refrigerate for approximately 4 hours.

2. For smoking on a gas grill, drain the wings from the brine and rinse. Sprinkle both sides lightly with the Sweet Heat Seasoning, and place the wings on a metal rack. Prepare a packet of wood chips by placing a few handfuls of chips on a large sheet of foil. Tightly seal up the foil, forming a rectangular packet, and poke several slits in the top. Turn the burner to medium on one side of the grill and place the packet directly over the flame. On the cold side of the grill, place the rack of wings. Close the grill cover and let smoke for 1 hour. Remove and keep warm. (Note: The wings will be lightly smoked, but not cooked through.)

3. For the wing glaze, in a large bowl, add the soy sauce, Worcestershire sauce, molasses, sriracha, sesame oil, ground ginger, chili powder, and minced garlic. Whisk to combine.

4. Preheat the oven to 400°F (200°C). Line a baking sheet with parchment paper.

5. Spread the wings on the prepared baking sheet, skin-side down. Brush the glaze on one side and then turn the wings to skin-side up and brush again. Place the tray on the top rack of the oven and bake for 30 minutes. Remove from the oven and brush the tops of the wings with more of the glaze, place back into the oven, and increase the temperature to 450°F (230°C). Watch carefully and let the wings cook until they begin to darken on top, 15 to 20 minutes. Remove and keep warm until ready to serve.

6. To serve, brush the tops of the wings with more glaze. (There will be leftover glaze; save for grilled pork chops or ribs.) Lightly sprinkle the wings with the sesame seeds and green onion. Serve the wings family style with the tray in the middle of the table or mound a scoop of brown rice in a bowl and stack a portion of wings on top for each guest.

OYSTER-STUFFED MUSHROOMS

These mushrooms are the stuff of dreams. The earthiness of these mushrooms with a rich creamy, liqueur-infused spinach stuffing spiked with fresh Gulf oysters and a pungent hit of herbs sends me into a dream state. The spice along with jalapeño-laced pepper Jack cheese balance the richness of this dish, which is crowned with a regal topping of grated Parmesan. Oh, yes!

8 large button mushrooms or baby portobellos

1 tablespoon (15 ml) olive oil

3 cups (90 g) tightly packed fresh spinach, stems removed

2 tablespoons (30 ml) Lillet or anise-flavored liqueur such as Pernod (optional)

½ cup (120 ml) heavy cream

1 cup (120 g) grated pepper Jack cheese

8 oysters with their liquor

1 teaspoon Cajun Seasoning Blend (page 231)

Dash of hot sauce

Kosher salt and freshly ground black pepper

1 tablespoon (8 g) cornstarch, if needed

¼ cup (25 g) grated Parmesan cheese

1. Inspect the mushrooms and clean them, removing the center stem and exposing the cavity.

2. In a skillet over medium-high heat, add the olive oil. Chop the spinach, add to the pan, and stir until it wilts, about 5 minutes.

3. Add the liqueur (if using) and cook off the alcohol, about 3 minutes. Add the cream and watch as it begins to reduce. Once it reduces by half, about 5 minutes, lower the heat to a simmer, and add the pepper Jack cheese.

4. Move the oysters to a cutting board, retaining the oyster liquor. Chop the oysters and add to the pan, along with 2 tablespoons (30 ml) of the oyster liquor. Continue simmering until the oysters are cooked through and the cream thickens, 5 to 8 minutes. Season with the Cajun seasoning, hot sauce, salt, and pepper.

5. If the mixture is not thick, sprinkle the cornstarch over the pan and stir until it becomes thick like stuffing. Move the pan off the heat and let cool.

6. Spoon the mixture into the cavity of the mushrooms and mound it on top. At this point, you can move the mushrooms to the refrigerator and chill until ready to bake.

7. Preheat the oven to 350°F (180°C).

8. In an ovenproof skillet or on a baking sheet, place the mushrooms and sprinkle with the Parmesan cheese. Bake on the center rack for 20 minutes. Serve immediately.

CRAWFISH DIP IN A FRENCH BREAD SKILLET

I stumbled on this combination when I was experimenting with store-bought pastry dough; it sparked my culinary creativity and this unique party recipe. The piping-hot rolls, buttered and sprinkled with Parmesan, are ablaze with spicy flavor when topped with the creamy crawfish dip.

DIP

½ cup (120 g) unsalted butter

1 cup (160 g) diced yellow onion

¼ cup (35 g) diced green bell pepper

¼ cup (35 g) diced red bell pepper

½ cup (60 g) diced celery

½ cup (35 g) chopped mushrooms

1½ teaspoons minced garlic

1 tablespoon (8 g) Cajun Seasoning Blend (page 231)

½ cup (120 ml) dry sherry

2 tablespoons (30 g) sour cream

½ cup (120 g) cream cheese

¼ cup (60 ml) heavy cream

1 pound (455 g) Louisiana crawfish tail meat (see Sources, page 232)

½ teaspoon cayenne pepper

Kosher salt and freshly ground black pepper

Dash of hot sauce

BREAD

All-purpose flour, for dusting

2 (11-ounce [308 g]) cans refrigerated French bread dough, such as Pillsbury

4 tablespoons (60 g) unsalted butter, melted

Kosher salt

2 tablespoons (10 g) grated Parmesan cheese

DIP

1. In a large cast-iron skillet over medium-high heat, melt the butter. Add the onion, bell peppers, celery, and mushrooms and sauté until the onion turns translucent, about 5 minutes. Add the garlic and Cajun seasoning, lower the heat to a simmer, and stir to combine. Add the sherry and cook for 5 minutes. Add the sour cream and cream cheese and stir until the cheese melts and thickens. Add the cream and continue stirring until it becomes the consistency of a dip, about 5 minutes.

2. Add the crawfish tail meat; stir the mixture to combine. Simmer the mixture for 10 minutes. Add the cayenne and season to taste with salt, pepper, and hot sauce. Keep warm for serving.

BREAD

1. Preheat the oven to 350°F (180°C). Coat a 10-inch (25 cm) cast-iron skillet with nonstick spray.

2. Sprinkle flour over a cutting board and remove the bread dough from the packages. Cut the rolled dough into 12 to 14 equal segments of about 2½ inches (6.4 cm). Roll on the cutting board with the palm of your hand until shaped into balls.

3. Add the dough balls along the perimeter of the prepared skillet, leaving a circular space in the middle. Brush the tops of the dough with the melted butter and place in the hot oven. Bake until golden brown, about 30 minutes. Remove from the oven, brush with more butter, and sprinkle with salt and the Parmesan cheese.

4. To serve, pour the hot crawfish dip into the hole in the middle of the French bread skillet. Serve family style in the middle of the table and invite your guests to pull apart the bread and dip it into the hot dip. Be sure to have plenty of napkins.

NOTES The number of French bread rounds will be dependent on the diameter of your skillet, so measure accordingly. Crawfish is excellent for this dip, but shrimp or crabmeat will work, too.

SWEET POTATO BREAD

Moist and flavorful with a slight sweetness, this is the perfect breakfast bread or afternoon treat. With a slather of sweet potato butter, it delivers a wallop of flavor. And the best part is it's quick and convenient. This is my version of a popular recipe hack that uses ice cream as the base, and when I saw all the Louisiana sweet potatoes stacked up in the produce bin at my local produce market, I was inspired.

Butter pecan ice cream is the surprise ingredient that makes this dish simple. This flavored ice cream already has butter, pecans, eggs, and milk as its base, and when combined with self-rising flour, it transforms into a loaf of bread just waiting to slide into the oven. I add a handful of pecans along with the mashed sweet potato for an infusion of down-home bayou flavor. It's just that easy.

3 cups (360 g) self-rising flour

2 cups (480 g) butter pecan ice cream, melted

1 cup (240 g) plus 2 tablespoons (30 g) mashed sweet potato puree, from baked sweet potatoes, divided

½ cup (70 g) chopped pecans

½ cup (120 g) unsalted butter, at room temperature

1. Preheat the oven to 350°F (180°C). Spray a 9 x 5-inch (23 x 12.7 cm) (or similar size) nonstick loaf pan with nonstick spray.

2. In a large mixing bowl, add the flour, ice cream, 1 cup (240 g) of the sweet potato puree, and pecans and stir to combine. Pour into the loaf pan and smooth out the top. Bake for 1 hour or until golden brown. Use a bamboo skewer to test for doneness; remove and let cool before slicing.

3. In a small bowl, combine the butter and remaining 2 tablespoons (30 g) sweet potato puree and scoop into a dish.

4. Slice and serve the bread with sweet potato butter on the side.

NOTES Cook time does not include baking the sweet potatoes. Bake your sweet potatoes ahead of time and be sure to mash or process the pulp until it is a smooth puree. Try this ice cream–based recipe for banana bread (banana ice cream and mashed bananas) or rum raisin bread (rum raisin ice cream, golden raisins and a splash of rum).

MUSHROOM AND PEPPER BREAD PUDDING

Earthy flavors grab my attention and draw me into a dark and delicious place that I find spellbinding. Such is my fascination with mushrooms that I forage for them in the wild, stalk them in the farmers' markets, and am delighted to see them in the supermarket aisles. This dish is perfect as a brunch entrée, a light dinner with a salad, or a side dish. Similar to a quiche or a tart, the soufflé-like, lighter-than-air texture gives lift to the elegance of the dish. It is based on a savory bread pudding with an all-vegetarian delivery of flavor. And with the hearty mushrooms taking center stage you will never miss the meat.

3 large eggs, beaten

1½ cups (360 ml) whole milk

½ teaspoon dried oregano

½ teaspoon dried thyme

Kosher salt and freshly ground black pepper

3 cups (300 g) cubed potato or brioche bread, crusts removed

1 pound (455 g) fresh mushrooms

3 large multicolored bell peppers

1 medium red onion

1. Preheat the oven to 350°F (180°C). Coat a 9 x 9-inch (23 x 23 cm) baking dish with nonstick spray. Line a baking sheet with foil.

2. In a large mixing bowl, add the eggs and milk and whisk to combine. Season the mixture with the herbs, a pinch of salt, and a grind of pepper. Add the bread cubes and submerge in the mixture; let sit for 10 minutes to soak up the liquid.

3. Inspect the mushrooms and clean them (do not wash) with a damp towel to remove any dirt. Slice them into large bite-size chunks.

4. Remove the stem and seeds from the bell peppers and slice into large bite-size chunks. Peel the onion and slice into large chunks.

5. In a microwavable dish with a lid, place the mushrooms, peppers, and onions. Coat with nonstick spray and lightly sprinkle with salt and pepper. Cover loosely with the lid and microwave on high for 5 minutes or just until the water releases from the mushrooms and all the vegetables wilt.

6. Add the vegetables to the egg mixture and stir combine. Pour into the prepared baking dish and spread the mixture to the edges. Place the baking dish on the prepared baking sheet and place in the oven. Bake until the egg custard mixture sets firmly and the top browns, about 1 hour. (Test for doneness by shaking the dish to see that the custard is set or prod it with a toothpick to see that it comes out clean.)

7. Remove from the oven and let rest before serving.

SMOTHERED GREEN BEANS WITH ANDOUILLE SAUSAGE

This green bean recipe is the one you'll always see on our holiday table. It's simply beans straight out of a can, but it's uncanny how these green beans—sautéed in smoky bacon grease, smothered in spicy andouille, and spiked with Cajun seasonings—will bring "thanks" to your Thanksgiving table.

This side dish is down-home fare often seen on a meat-and-three plate most anywhere in rural Louisiana. In fact, a Creole cook at a steam table lunchroom in Evangeline Parish spilled the beans on the list of ingredients in this casserole combination. You might think that fresh green beans would enhance this recipe, but I promise you they won't. Canned green beans have both the taste and the texture that define this dish, which is even better made a day or two in advance.

8 strips smoked bacon, chopped

1 cup (140 g) loosely packed sliced andouille sausage (see Sources, page 232) or smoked pork sausage

½ cup (80 g) diced yellow onion

¼ cup (30 g) diced celery

2 tablespoons (20 g) diced red bell pepper

2 tablespoons (16 g) all-purpose flour

½ cup (120 ml) vegetable stock or chicken stock

1 (28-ounce [784 g]) can cut Italian green beans, such as Margaret Holmes brand, drained

1 teaspoon white pepper

1 teaspoon granulated garlic

1 teaspoon black pepper

1 teaspoon kosher salt

2 tablespoons (30 ml) heavy whipping cream

1. In a heavy skillet over medium heat, add the bacon and fry until browned and crisp, about 8 minutes. Remove the bacon pieces and drain on a paper towel.

2. In the same skillet, add the andouille, onion, celery, and red bell pepper to the remaining grease, and cook until the sausage browns on both sides. Sprinkle the flour over the pan and stir it into the remaining grease to make a roux. Cook, stirring, until the flour begins to turn a beige color, about 5 minutes. Add the stock, stir for 5 minutes until it thickens, and then add the green beans. Stir to combine and season with the white pepper, granulated garlic, black pepper, and salt. Add the heavy cream and stir to combine. Lower the heat and let simmer and thicken for 5 minutes. Turn off the heat and keep warm.

3. Just before serving, sprinkle the top of the green beans with the crisp bacon pieces.

SHRIMP RISOTTO

Creamy risotto perfumed with fresh herbs, slow-simmered in wine, elevated with briny wild-caught shrimp from the waters off the Gulf Coast, and finished with delicate pecan oil is delicious perfection in my food world. Serve with hot bread and wine.

6 cups (1.4 L) fish or shrimp stock

1 pound (455 g) extra-large (21/25 count) raw shrimp, deveined with shells removed

1 teaspoon Cajun Seasoning Blend (page 231)

2 tablespoons (30 g) unsalted butter, divided

2 tablespoons (30 ml) pecan or olive oil, divided

1 large yellow onion, finely diced

2 ribs celery, finely diced

1 teaspoon minced garlic

1½ cups (250 g) Arborio rice

1 cup (240 ml) dry white wine

1 large lemon

1 tablespoon (3 g) chopped fresh flat-leaf parsley

1 tablespoon (3 g) chopped fresh rosemary

½ cup (30 g) fresh basil leaves, stems removed

Kosher salt and freshly ground black pepper

1. Place the stock in a pot and keep warm at a low simmer.

2. Butterfly the shrimp by slicing vertically along the inside to open up the shrimp, and sprinkle with the Cajun seasoning.

3. In a saucepan over medium heat, add 1 tablespoon (15 g) of the butter. When hot, add the shrimp. Sauté the shrimp until they begin to color, about 3 minutes. Remove from the heat and set aside.

4. In a large heavy pot over medium-high heat, melt the remaining 1 tablespoon (15 g) butter and add 1 tablespoon (15 ml) of the pecan oil. Add the onion, celery, and garlic and sauté for 1 minute. Add the rice and stir until the rice begins to toast, about 3 minutes. Add the wine and stir until it is absorbed, about 5 minutes, then lower the heat to a simmer.

5. With a grater, remove the zest from the lemon and save for later use. Slice the lemon in half and squeeze the juice from half a lemon into the pot, being careful to catch any seeds.

6. Add 1 ladle of the simmering fish stock and stir until absorbed, about 5 minutes. For a total cooking time of about 30 minutes, continue stirring the rice in 5-minute intervals and adding liquid (1 ladle at a time) as needed as it soaks it up. Be sure to scrape the sides of the pot and keep any rice from sticking.

7. Add the shrimp to the pot along with the reserved lemon zest, parsley, rosemary, and basil, and cook for another 5 minutes. As the risotto becomes creamy, sample the rice to make sure it is fully cooked and adjust the seasoning with salt and pepper. Just before serving, stir in the remaining 1 tablespoon (15 ml) pecan oil.

8. Serve in shallow bowls.

BEER-BRAISED BEEF STEW

Explore new tastes with this easy recipe—a dark and mysterious combination of sirloin beef cooked down in beer for a magical dish that will add spice to your Louisiana recipe repertoire.

1 tablespoon (15 ml) vegetable oil

2 pounds (910 g) lean top sirloin beef, cut into cubes

1 cup (160 g) roughly chopped yellow onion

1 cup (120 g) roughly chopped celery

1 cup (150 g) roughly chopped green bell pepper

1 tablespoon (15 g) tomato paste

2 tablespoons (16 g) all-purpose flour

½ cup (25 g) chopped flat-leaf parsley

1 tablespoon (3 g) chopped fresh rosemary

1 tablespoon (8 g) minced garlic

1 (12-ounce [360 ml]) bottle dark beer

4 cups (960 ml) beef stock

½ teaspoon cayenne pepper

½ teaspoon smoked paprika

Kosher salt and freshly ground black pepper

1 bay leaf

1 large russet potato, peeled and cut into large chunks

2 large carrots, peeled and roughly chopped

1 tablespoon (15 g) unsalted butter

1 tablespoon (8 g) all-purpose flour, if needed

6 cups (1.2 kg) cooked long-grain white rice

1 cup (100 g) diced green onion tops, for garnish

1. In a cast-iron pot with a heavy lid over medium-high heat, add the oil. Once the oil is smoking hot, add the cubes of beef (don't crowd the pot) and brown on both sides, about 8 minutes. Remove each batch of beef to a platter and keep warm.

2. Add the onion, celery, and bell pepper, and cook until the onion turns translucent, about 5 minutes. Add the tomato paste and cook for another 2 minutes. Add the flour to the vegetable mixture and stir while cooking the raw taste from the flour, about 3 minutes.

3. Add the parsley, rosemary, and garlic and deglaze the pot with the beer. Add the beef back to the pot along with the stock and stir, scraping the bits from the bottom of the pot.

4. Season with the cayenne, paprika, salt, and pepper and add the bay leaf to the pot. Cover and simmer for 1 hour.

5. Add the chunks of potato and carrot and cook covered for another 1 hour.

6. Uncover and taste the stew for spice and thickness. Season with salt and pepper if needed, remove the bay leaf, and add the knob of butter just before serving to add flavor and sheen to the gravy. If you want your stew thicker, make a quick beurre manié by blending the flour with the butter and adding it to the pot. Once it comes to a boil, it will thicken. The stew should be thick enough to coat the back of a spoon.

7. Serve in bowls over a mound of white rice. Garnish with the diced green onion.

OYSTER PASTA

This white sauce is a rich and delicate stage for its star ingredients. Smoky andouille builds the lower bass notes while fresh spinach leaves along with fresh Gulf oysters elevate the elegance of this Creole recipe. Heavy cream and a sprinkling of freshly grated Parmigiano-Reggiano cheese bring it all together and translate this into one spectacular dish.

½ cup (144 g) table salt

1 (16-ounce [455 g]) package pappardelle pasta or wide pasta noodles

2 tablespoons (30 ml) vegetable oil

2 cups (280 g) sliced smoked andouille sausage (see Sources, page 232)

1 cup (160 g) diced yellow onion

½ cup (60 g) diced celery

½ cup (75 g) diced red bell pepper

½ cup (75 g) diced yellow bell pepper

1 tablespoon (8 g) minced garlic

2 tablespoons (6 g) chopped
fresh rosemary

½ cup (120 ml) dry white wine

2 cups (60 g) fresh spinach leaves,
stems removed

4 cups (960 ml) heavy cream

1 tablespoon (8 g) Cajun Seasoning
Blend (page 231)

Dash of hot sauce

1 pint (455 g) Louisiana Gulf oysters,
with oyster liquor

½ cup (50 g) freshly grated Parmigiano-
Reggiano cheese

½ cup (50 g) diced green onion tops

Kosher salt

French bread, for serving

1. Fill a large pot with water and add the table salt. Place over high heat and bring to a boil. Add the pasta and cook until just al dente. Remove from the heat and strain. Reserve for later use.

2. In a large pan with a tight-fitting lid over medium-high heat, add the oil. Add the sausage, onion, celery, and bell peppers and cook until the onion turns translucent, about 5 minutes. Add the garlic, rosemary, white wine, and spinach and stir to combine. Let the alcohol burn off as the spinach begins to wilt. Add the cream and stir. Decrease the heat to a simmer, cover the pan, and cook for 15 minutes, stirring every 5 minutes.

3. Uncover the pan and stir. The spinach should be wilted and the cream will have begun to reduce. Continue simmering the mixture as the sauce thickens. Add the Cajun seasoning and hot sauce to taste. Turn off the heat until ready to serve.

4. Chop half the oysters and leave the remaining oysters whole. Just before serving, bring the cream and spinach mixture back to a simmer and add the oysters and ¼ cup (60 ml) of the oyster liquor. Gently simmer the oysters in the creamy bath until they are delicately poached and the edges begin to curl and wrinkle, about 5 minutes.

5. Add the precooked pasta and simmer until the pasta is fully cooked, about 5 minutes. Add the cheese and green onions and stir into the sauce. Turn off the heat. Taste and add kosher salt, if needed.

6. Serve the pasta in shallow bowls with crusty French bread for dipping in the rich sauce.

MEMORIES ON THE HALF SHELL

My daddy was an oyster man. Oh, I don't mean a fisherman who plies his trade harvesting sack after sack of fresh oysters from Louisiana's Gulf waters, but rather, my dad was obsessed with eating them. Baked oysters, fried oysters, oyster stew, and oyster po'boys were all part of my dad's oyster addiction, but if you want to know his favorite way of eating oysters, just read on.

When I was old enough to appreciate the difference between fish sticks and trout Amandine, my father loaded me into his pickup early one Saturday morning and took me on an adventure. From my home in the small Louisiana town of Bogalusa, the city of New Orleans was just an hour away and a world apart. That day spent with my dad was my culinary epiphany; it was an awakening that sent me on the path of delicious discovery that I still walk to this day. Here's the story in a nutshell. . . uh, half shell.

Once a month, my father visited a restaurant supply wholesaler to buy kitchen appliances and other provisions for his café, and on occasion, I tagged along. He was deep in thought that morning, and we barely spoke as we trucked along the two-lane blacktop road that wound through Bush, over Money Hill, and into Mandeville. But when we started across the twenty-six-mile-long causeway bridging Lake Pontchartrain to New Orleans, he started talking a blue streak.

As is usual in my family, the conversation soon turned to food. He began to rant about the high price of beef and other meats, and as he looked out across the lake and saw the crab boats motoring along their line of traps, he proclaimed he might change to an all-seafood menu. He asked what my favorite was, and I didn't hesitate to volunteer my preference for fried shrimp, which I knew would be on his new menu. Somewhere in the conversation, before we exited the bridge, he mentioned oysters, and I told him I had never eaten one of those slimy things and couldn't see why anyone else would either. With a tilt of his head and a snide little smile, he acknowledged my critique. And he decided on lunch.

We finished up at the supply store by mid-morning, and he drove a beeline to the French Quarter. My father parked the truck in the parking garage in the Monteleone Hotel and quickly ushered me onto the street. "Gotta beat the crowd," he said, and we walked at a half-trot down Iberville Street to what I was about to find out was his holy shrine of deliciousness.

Scurrying by storefronts and shuffling past leisurely tourists, we stopped abruptly. We had arrived. I wasn't quite sure what this place was, why I was there, or why he was so anxious for me to see it. I surveyed the outside and what I saw with my untrained eye was just another dilapidated building with a neon sign that read Felix's Restaurant. And then, I saw a big smile on his face. There on the sign along the bottom row, I read "oysters."

Five decades later, I am now firmly convinced that while my father waited at the pearly gates to see St. Peter, he downed a couple dozen of those salty wonders that he swore were never as good anywhere else as at Felix's Oyster Bar. His devotion to this little joint was borderline fanatical, and his passion for oysters is a bona fide obsession. As I would come to find out, mine would be too.

He opened the glass door, and the blast of cold air inside Felix's Oyster Bar was a welcome relief from my forced "death march" down the scorched cement sidewalks of the Quarter. I looked to see what table he would pick out for us and was surprised when he motioned me to jump up on a stool beside him at the bar. Back then, it was okay for underage kids to sip a Roy Rogers at the bar, but even I was shocked that we were at the bar at 11:30 a.m. As you might have guessed, this was an oyster bar, and when I looked over the counter at the ice-filled metal bin stacked high with oyster shells, I knew it was an adventure I wouldn't soon forget.

Daddy got a bottle of Jax (it's never too early with oysters), and I took a swig of my Barq's. My father held up two fingers, and the man behind the counter went to work. Our shucker could dispatch a couple dozen fresh out of their shells before you could mix up your bowl of sauce. And speaking of sauce, my father had a particular combination that took full advantage of everything offered. It was always ketchup at the base, a bit of Blue Plate, a glob of horseradish, a shot of Worcestershire, a squeeze of lemon, and a dash or three of Tabasco–pungent to say the least. I took charge of my personal sauce detail and went easier on the hot stuff.

There's nothing too terribly difficult about eating an oyster. My dad subscribes to the "sauce, slurp, and sip" method of stabbing an oyster for a quick plunge in his spicy sauce cauldron and swallowing it whole with a beer chaser. I, however, went cracker-style by placing an oyster on a saltine with a spoonful of sauce and placing the entire thing in my mouth. By the time I slid down the last of my dozen, they tasted pretty darn good.

By the end of the second dozen, I was becoming quite the expert, hanging shell-for-shell with him. At that time in my life, there had been only one occasion (coming runner-up in the Cub Scouts'

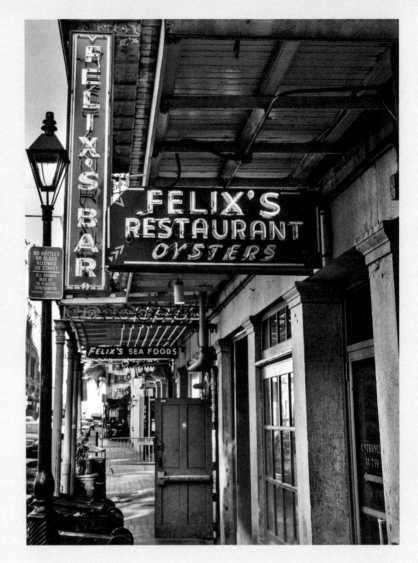

Pinewood Derby) where I had impressed my father. This was the second. He would later tell me on the ride home that when I finished off that third dozen, he knew for sure that I was his son and that he was most proud of me. I glowed. Either from the lofty praise of my proud father or the horseradish, I glowed.

As I look back, I can tell that day spent with my dad at Felix's Oyster Bar was more than a platter of oysters. That day was a rite of passage of my father welcoming me into his world. Some kids learn a perfect curveball or how to rapid fire a 12-gauge at a flock of oncoming geese, but I learned to lock and load three dozen oysters balanced on a barstool at nine years old.

Not too shabby.

RAW OYSTER RULES

It's all about raw oysters, and instead of a recipe, let's have a kitchen table conversation. I'll start it off with what I call my "rules" when it comes to eating oysters, and I'll condense them down to seven points.

1. FRESH GULF OYSTERS ARE THE BEST

I know that other parts of the country have tasty oysters, but being born and fed in Louisiana, I swear by the briny bivalves that come out of our Gulf of Mexico waters. Plump and not too sweet, these Atlantic species of oysters are consistently larger than others.

2. TIME OF YEAR

Oyster lore of long ago was that you only eat oysters in a month that has an "R" in it. September through April being the cooler months during which the oysters were at their peak. With modern harvesting, processing, and cold storage, that is no longer the case. All that said, there are still many who subscribe to that belief and shun raw oysters during the heat of the summer months of July and August. I'm one of them. The real reason is that these months are the spawning season and the oysters tend to be watery and not at their tastiest.

3. SHUCK 'EM TO ORDER

Unless you are a do-it-yourself home shucker, your choice of restaurant will be important. Go to an establishment that has an honest-to-goodness stand-up oyster bar with fresh raw oysters on ice. And strike up a conversation with the oyster shuckers; they are a rich source of information. Pass on any restaurant that serves their oysters on a tray out of the back kitchen. And always tip your oyster shucker before he begins shucking; you'll always get his best oysters and service.

4. ORDER UP A DOZEN AT A TIME

Order one dozen oysters for yourself. Why bother with anything less? But by ordering just a dozen, you can check out the plumpness, taste the brininess, and determine if this oyster purveyor is worth his salt. Another dozen, please.

5. GET SAUCY

Lots of purists scoff at sauce with their oysters, but I enjoy the spike of spice that sauce adds to the experience of eating raw oysters. While you wait for your tray of oysters, make your sauce from the usual ingredients (ketchup, horseradish, Worcestershire, hot sauce, and lemon). If they do not have an add-on you like, then feel free to ask.

6. THE LITTLE FORK

The primary function of the small cocktail fork is to pull and scrape the oyster muscle from the shell if the shucker hasn't done his job correctly (which is rare). Most experienced oyster eaters will discard the fork and simply squeeze a little lemon and a drop of hot sauce, slurp the oyster from the shell, and let it slide. The reason for this is simple: oyster liquor. The natural juice in an oyster is fresh and briny with a texture all its own. But if you are a novice, feel free to spear your oyster with the fork, drag it through the sauce, and bring it to your open mouth. Either way, it works.

7. CRACKER OR NO CRACKER?

Pros forgo the saltines, but most amateur oyster eaters (me included) enjoy the crunchy platform that salted cracker squares provide in staging the oyster. But by no means should you ever take out a knife and fork. No matter how large the oyster, it is supposed to be consumed whole.

And that's that. Nothing to cook here. Pull up a stool, pop open a cold one, order up a dozen raw, and make a few memories on the half shell.

CAJUN PIG ROAST

Fall-apart tender roast pig with a layer of crackling skin is the iconic *cochon de lait*, a Louisiana culinary event that is full of flavor and French tradition. Cooking a whole pig is not especially tricky, but it does require some special equipment: the Cajun microwave. Based on the acclaimed La Caja China pig-roasting box, the Cajun microwave is a Louisiana version where an insulated cooking chamber is covered with a layer of hot embers of charcoal and wood chunks (see Sources, page 232).

The prep is simple with an overnight injectable marinade, but the 10- to 12-hour cooking time requires your full attention to keep the internal temperature constant and to prevent burning of the meat. It helps to have a friend (or two) assist. The skin is the prize: a cloak of crispy cracklin that comes off in chunks and is eaten alongside the succulent meat; this texture and taste combo is hard to beat. I like to serve this with green beans and paella rice on the side.

1 (40- to 50-pound [18.2 to 22.8 kg]) dressed whole pig, head and feet removed

2 cups (240 g) Cajun Seasoning Blend (page 231)

1 quart (960 ml) apple cider

1 tablespoon (18 g) table salt

1 tablespoon (8 g) black pepper

1 tablespoon (6 g) garlic powder

1. The day before, move the pig to a cutting board and season the inside of the pig liberally with Cajun seasoning or have your butcher preseason the meat.

2. In a large container, combine the apple cider, salt, pepper, and garlic powder. Fill an injector needle with the solution and inject the meat all over until you have penetrated all the major muscles. Pour any of the leftover marinade into a metal loaf pan. Wrap the pig in foil, place it in a large ice chest, and cover with ice. Let chill overnight.

3. Early the next morning, remove the pig from the ice chest and let it come to room temperature, still wrapped in foil.

4. Thoroughly clean and prepare a Cajun microwave cooker with coals (charcoal and wood chunks) until the internal temperature of the box comes to 250°F (120°C). Place the pig in the box skin-side down (rib cage facing up) and place the pan of leftover marinade in the box for added moisture as it evaporates. Place the hot coal-laden cover on top and let cook for 6 hours. Be sure to watch your thermometer and keep the temperature at a consistent 250°F (120°C) by adding more charcoal or wood chunks to the fire.

5. After 6 hours, uncover, remove the foil, and with the help of a friend and using heatproof gloves, turn the pig over so it is skin-side up. During this second half of the cook time, the skin and back fat crisp and crack, so be sure to keep the temperature up to 250°F (120°C). Replace the cover and cook for an additional 6 hours or until the skin crisps and the meat is pull-apart tender. Check periodically during cooking and if the pig is cooking too hot or you detect burning, loosely cover the meat with heavy-duty aluminum foil.

6. After the full 12-hour cooking time, remove the pig, cover and keep warm with aluminum foil, and let rest until serving.

7. To serve, use a sharp knife or cleaver to cut through the crispy skin and remove it in chunks to a pan. Cut down through the backbone and ribs to expose the meat. Pull the meat apart into pieces, discarding any excess fat. Serve your guests family style.

NOTE Prep time does not include marinade time.

PORK BELLY PORCHETTA

Italian butchers are experts at preparing pork, and their specialty porchetta redefines the pig-eating experience. Make no mistake, this recipe is not for dainty diners or novice eaters who aren't willing to work for an amazing meat-eating experience. This is big pig: An 8½-pound (3.8 kg) pork belly stuffed, rolled, tied, and roasted to crispy perfection. I like to roast potatoes in the pork belly pan drippings for the perfect side.

1 (8½-pound [3.8 kg]) whole boneless pork belly, fat and skin attached

Kosher salt and freshly ground black pepper

2 tablespoons (16 g) Cajun Seasoning Blend (page 231)

6 tablespoons (50 g) minced garlic

½ cup (80 g) finely diced onion

¼ cup (30 g) finely diced celery

¼ cup (35 g) finely diced red or green bell pepper

½ cup (25 g) chopped fresh flat-leaf parsley

¼ cup (12 g) packed fresh sage leaves, stems removed

2 tablespoons (6 g) chopped fresh rosemary

1 large fennel bulb, fronds attached

1. On a cutting board, lay out the pork belly fat-side down and sprinkle generously with salt and pepper. Spread the Cajun seasoning and minced garlic evenly over the meat, stopping 2 inches (5 cm) short of the edges.

2. Sprinkle the onion, celery, and bell pepper evenly across the surface of the meat, and add the parsley, sage, and rosemary.

3. Break the fronds off the fennel bulb and spread them across the center of the pork belly.

4. Grab the outer edge of the meat and roll it up, encasing the stuffing inside (you will lose some of the stuffing). Be sure to roll it tightly. Working from the end, tie the meat tightly every 2 inches (5 cm) with a double knot. When finished, neatly snip the ends of the twine.

5. Place the pork on a rack set atop a large rimmed baking sheet lined with aluminum foil. Place in the refrigerator overnight to marinate and infuse the flavors into the meat.

6. Preheat the oven to 325°F (170°C).

7. Place the porchetta into the oven on the center rack and add 2 cups (480 ml) of water to the bottom of the tray. Cook uncovered until the internal temperature of the pork reaches 145°F (63°C) on a meat thermometer, 2 to 3 hours. Remove from the oven and cover with foil to rest for about 10 minutes. The carryover cooking will allow the interior temperature of the meat to increase about 10°F (5°C) to 155°F (68°C).

8. At this point, you can hold the porchetta until ready to finish once your guests arrive.

9. When ready to serve, increase the temperature of the oven to 500°F (250°C) and continue cooking as the outer skin turns golden brown and begins to crisp, 20 to 30 minutes. Watch carefully to prevent burning.

10. Check the internal temperature of the pork again and it should now register from 165° to 175°F (74° to 80°C), an ideal temperature.

11. Cover the porchetta with aluminum foil and let rest for at least 10 minutes before slicing.

12. Remove the string, and cut the porchetta into thick slices.

NOTES I know what you're thinking: Will that bad boy fit into my oven? I have a large oven space that accommodates my pork belly, but if you do not, cut the roast in half and cook together on the same tray.

BACON-WRAPPED CHICKEN THIGH STUFFED WITH SPINACH AND ARTICHOKE WITH A PEPPER JELLY GLAZE

Chicken thighs for dinner? Boring! But how about amping up the flavor a notch or two? If wrapping a meaty chicken thigh with smoky bacon wasn't enough, then stuff it with spinach and artichoke and glaze it all with spicy pepper jelly. Oh yeah, now we're talking.

1 tablespoon (15 g) unsalted butter

½ cup (80 g) finely diced yellow onion

1 teaspoon minced garlic

1 (8-ounce [227 g]) bag fresh baby spinach leaves

1 (14-ounce [392 g]) can artichoke hearts packed in water, drained

2 tablespoons (16 g) all-purpose flour

½ cup (60 g) grated Monterey Jack cheese

2 tablespoons (30 ml) heavy cream

1 teaspoon white pepper

Kosher salt and freshly ground black pepper

4 large boneless, skinless chicken thighs

1 tablespoon (8 g) Cajun Seasoning Blend (page 231)

4 strips smoked bacon

½ cup (120 g) pepper jelly

1. In a large skillet with a tight-fitting lid over medium-high heat, add the butter. Sauté the onion until it turns translucent, about 5 minutes. Add the garlic and cook another minute.

2. Add the spinach leaves and the artichoke hearts. Add a bit (¼ cup (60 ml)) of water to create steam and close the lid. Watch as the steam escapes and cook for 5 minutes until the liquid is gone.

3. Open the lid and stir the mixture, breaking down the artichoke hearts with the back of a spatula or fork.

4. Sprinkle the flour over the mixture. Cook until the raw flour taste is removed, about 3 minutes.

5. Add the cheese and cream, and season with white pepper, salt, and black pepper.

6. Continue stirring until the mixture thickens to a stuffing consistency. Remove from the heat and refrigerate for 1 hour or until ready to use.

7. Preheat the oven to 350°F (180°C).

8. Remove the chicken thighs to a cutting board and, using a sharp paring knife, enlarge the pocket inside each thigh. Season the meat with a sprinkle of Cajun seasoning.

9. Using a spoon (or your fingers) pack in the chilled stuffing.

10. Close the flaps of the chicken and use toothpicks to hold in place.

11. Wrap the bacon tightly around the meat.

12. Place the chicken on a wire rack suspended over a baking tray, and move to the oven to bake for 40 minutes until the bacon is browned. Check the temperature with an instant-read thermometer; it should register 175°F (80°C) in the thickest part of the thigh meat.

13. Remove the chicken and brush on the pepper jelly. Move the baking tray back to the upper rack of the oven and turn the temperature to broil. Watch carefully as the glaze sets and the bacon crisps, 1 to 2 minutes.

14. Remove the chicken and serve with extra pepper jelly on the side.

NOTES If your chicken thighs are small, use two and hold them together with toothpicks. Use regular bacon, not the thick-cut version since you want it to cook quickly and seal the exterior of the chicken. I've made these thighs as both an entrée and as an appetizer; I cut them in half as a party starter. The stuffing options are endless: boudin and pepper Jack, broccoli and cheddar, or Italian sausage and mozzarella are just a few.

SMOTHERED SEVEN STEAK IN ONION GRAVY

The deep, dark onion gravy that suspends this fall-apart tender beef is draped across a mountain of long-grain white rice; it is an ascent into the heavens of Louisiana cooking. Seven steak is a classic of rural roots recipes, and you can find it on most farmhouse tables and lunchroom steam tables alike. Break out the yeast rolls and pour a glass of sweet tea, because this is Cajun cooking at its best. Traditionally this dish is always served over rice, but it would be tasty over mashed potatoes, too.

2 tablespoons (30 ml) vegetable oil

2½ pounds (1.1 kg) seven steaks, bone in, ½ to ¾ inch (1.3 to 2 cm) thick

1 tablespoon (8 g) Cajun Seasoning Blend (page 231)

3 large yellow onions

6 cups (1.4 L) beef stock or water

3 tablespoons (45 ml) Dark Cajun Roux (page 230)

Kosher salt

6 cups (1.2 kg) cooked long-grain white rice, for serving

1. In a large cast-iron skillet (or pot) with a heavy lid over medium-high heat, add the oil. Sprinkle the seven steaks with the Cajun seasoning and place in the hot oil, searing both sides until browned, about 8 minutes. Cook in batches until all are browned and remove to a platter.

2. Peel and roughly chop one onion and slice the other two into rings. Add the onions to the pan and sauté until browned, about 7 minutes, and then add the stock and roux, stirring to combine.

3. Add the seven steaks back to the skillet and cover. Lower the heat to a simmer and cook on the stovetop for approximately 2 hours or until the meat is fork tender and the gravy thickens.

4. Taste the gravy and add salt if needed. Serve over a mound of white rice (or mashed potatoes).

WHAT IS A SEVEN STEAK?

It's an inexpensive center cut of bone-in chuck called a seven-bone pot roast because the bone is shaped like the number 7. Have the butcher cut it into steaks that are ½ inch to ¾ inch (1.3 to 2 cm) thick. When I say "steaks," don't mistake this for a cut of meat that you can grill like t-bone or ribeye. No, this is a tough cut of meat that needs a long braise in liquid or what a good Southern home cook refers to as "smothering." For the added flavor it brings to the pot, I like my seven steaks with the bone left in, which might take a little more searching since many contemporary big-city butchers like to remove the bone.

GUINEA GUMBO

I remember it like it was yesterday: the day, over 30 years ago, that I first tasted a guinea gumbo and was immediately initiated into the colorful world of Cajun cooking. So what does guinea hen taste like? The taste of guinea hens has more in common with wild game birds like pheasant than domestic poultry. It is a sublimely rich and gamey version of chicken. Guinea hen meat is leaner and a bit drier than chicken, so the cooking method almost always includes layers of flavor and a long, slow braise. Perfect for a guinea gumbo.

6 strips smoked bacon, chopped

1 whole guinea hen, cut into pieces (Sources, page 232)

1 tablespoon (8 g) Cajun Seasoning Blend (page 231)

2 cups (320 g) diced yellow onion

2 cups (300 g) diced green bell pepper

2 cups (240 g) diced celery

2 tablespoons (16 g) minced garlic

½ cup (25 g) chopped flat-leaf parsley

1 tablespoon (8 g) cayenne pepper

2 bay leaves

12 cups (2.9 L) dark chicken stock, plus more if needed

1 cup (240 ml) dark Cajun roux, plus more if needed (page 230)

3 links garlic smoked pork sausage

Kosher salt and freshly ground black pepper

Dash of hot sauce

8 cups (1.6 kg) cooked Louisiana long-grain white rice

1 cup (100 g) diced green onion tops

Filé powder, for serving

1. In a large cast-iron pot with a heavy lid over medium-high heat, add the bacon pieces and cook until fully rendered, about 8 minutes. Remove the bacon to a paper towel–lined plate. Pour off all but 2 tablespoons of the bacon fat and reserve the rest.

2. Sprinkle the guinea hen pieces with Cajun seasoning and place them into the hot fat. Brown on all sides for about 10 minutes, and remove to a platter.

3. In the same pot over medium-high heat, add more bacon grease, if needed, and then add the onions, bell pepper, and celery and cook until browned, about 8 minutes. Add the garlic, parsley, cayenne, and bay leaves, and stir. Add the guinea hen and the stock. Bring the pot to a simmer and add the roux. Place the whole sausage links along with the bacon pieces into the pot and immerse in the stock. Cover and simmer for 1 hour.

4. Uncover and stir. Skim the surface to remove any excess oil and discard. If it is too thick, add more stock. If it is too thin, add more roux. Add salt, pepper, and hot sauce to taste. Cover and cook on low for 1 more hour.

5. Uncover and skim the surface to remove excess oil. At this point, you can leave the guinea hen on the bone or debone it by removing the bones and skin from each of the pieces and adding the meat back to the pot. Remove the sausage links, slice them into bite-size pieces and return them to the pot. Cover and cook for another 30 minutes.

6. To serve, ladle the gumbo over white rice and serve with a sprinkle of diced green onion tops and filé powder on the side.

NOTES Substituting guinea hen with a stewing hen or rooster is acceptable, but the flavors will be much different. If you have trouble finding guinea hen, you can source the product online at Dartagnan.com (Sources, page 232).

COFFEE-RUBBED PRIME RIB

The juices from this prime rib, roasted to perfect pink, mingle with spicy seasonings and savory herbs to produce a heavenly jus. My secret weapon is coating the exterior with oil and my deep, dark coffee rub accented with grated lemon zest and chopped rosemary; this combination ensures a crusty exterior. And when bathed over roasted fingerling potatoes, this meat and potatoes combo is the foundation of a most elegant holiday dinner. For the requisite horseradish cream, blend equal parts prepared horseradish and mayonnaise.

COFFEE RUB

½ cup (65 g) dark roast whole bean coffee, finely ground

½ cup (115 g) dark brown sugar

½ cup (144 g) kosher salt

½ cup (48 g) garlic powder

½ cup (48 g) coarsely ground black pepper

PRIME RIB

1 (4½-pound [2 kg]) standing rib roast, trimmed and tied

1 pound (455 g) fingerling potatoes

2 tablespoons (30 ml) rendered beef fat or olive oil

Kosher salt and freshly ground black pepper

3 tablespoons (45 ml) olive oil

¼ cup (24 g) grated lemon zest

¼ cup (12 g) chopped fresh rosemary

COFFEE RUB

1. In a mixing bowl, add the coffee, brown sugar, salt, garlic powder, and pepper and mix well to combine evenly. Cover and set aside.

PRIME RIB

1. Take the roast out of the refrigerator 1 hour before cooking and let it come to room temperature.

2. Preheat the oven to 450°F (230°C).

3. Coat the potatoes in the rendered beef fat and lightly sprinkle with salt and pepper. Place the potatoes in the bottom of a large roasting pan and cover with a metal rack.

4. Rub the rib roast with the olive oil and sprinkle liberally with the coffee rub on all sides. Stand the roast up, bone-side down, and spread the lemon zest and rosemary over the top and sides. Insert a meat thermometer into the center of the roast (not touching a bone) and place the roast on the rack. Place the roasting pan containing the beef and potatoes into the hot oven and roast for 20 minutes, then lower the temperature to 275°F (140°C) and continue roasting until the meat thermometer registers 125°F (52°C), about 1 hour.

5. Remove the roast from the oven, place the prime rib on a serving tray, arrange the potatoes around it, and loosely cover with foil; let rest for 30 minutes.

6. For carving and serving, you have two options: You can slice away the bottom rib bones and lay the meat on top, slicing individual portions. Or I prefer to leave the prime rib on the bone where you have the option to slice a hefty bone-in portion. Served with beef fat–roasted potatoes, a little beef jus, and horseradish cream, this is a royal dinner, for sure.

NOTES Gauging the internal temperature of the meat is essential; I use both an oven meat probe thermometer with an alert, as well as an instant-read thermometer at the finish. A final temperature of 125°F (52°C) will carryover another five degrees which should yield a perfect medium-rare pink. If any of your guests prefer their beef cooked more, the end slices should be cooked to medium.

STUFFED DUCK WITH DUCK FAT ONIONS

Stuffing a fat duck with fresh green onion sausage combined with diced apple is simple enough, but slow roasting it until tender, broiling it for a crispy finish, and adding Vidalia onions to the jus to soak up the duck fat is sheer brilliance. This recipe is moist, tender, and bursting with layers of flavor, and when the sweet sugars of the Vidalias ooze their nectar, well I just run out of words. Best of all, it's just in time for your winter table.

STUFFING

2 pounds (910 g) bulk raw pork sausage, such as Cajun green onion sausage (see Sources, page 232)

1 medium apple, peeled, cored, and finely diced

½ cup (50 g) unseasoned bread crumbs

1 teaspoon black pepper

DUCK

1 (4- to 5-pound [1.8 to 2.2 kg]) Muscovy duck, cleaned

2 tablespoons (16 g) Cajun Seasoning Blend (page 231)

4 large whole Vidalia onions or any sweet onion, peeled and halved

1 cup (240 ml) water

1 tablespoon (15 ml) melted butter

STUFFING

1. In a mixing bowl, add the pork sausage (remove from the casing, if necessary). Add the apple, bread crumbs, and pepper and use your hands to combine.

DUCK

1. Preheat the oven to 350°F (180°C).

2. Inspect the duck and remove any remaining pinfeathers and the packet of organ meats in the cavity. Rinse the inside of the duck thoroughly. Sprinkle the cavity and all sides of the duck with the Cajun seasoning. Stuff the sausage/apple combination into the cavity.

3. In a large disposable aluminum foil baking pan with high sides, place the onions on the bottom flat-side up. Top with a wire rack and place the stuffed duck on top. Using the sharp point of a wooden skewer, repeatedly poke holes in the surface fat and skin of the duck on the top, bottom, and all sides, but do not pierce all the way to the meat. Add the water to the bottom of the pan and cook uncovered (repeat the pricking of the skin/fat at about the halfway point of cooking) until the duck juices run clear and the internal temperature of the duck (thigh portion) and the stuffing reaches 175°F (80°C), 1½ to 2 hours.

4. Remove the foil roasting pan from the oven and set the oven to high broil. Move the cooked duck to a clean baking sheet. Remove the onions from the roasting pan and place on a wire rack for 5 minutes to drain excess duck fat, and then place them alongside the duck on the baking sheet.

5. Just before serving, brush the top of the duck with the butter and run under the broiler for a minute or so until the skin begins to brown and crisp (watch carefully to prevent burning). Remove the duck and onions, place on a platter, and serve family style in the center of the table. Carve the duck into pieces and serve with the stuffing and onions.

ROASTED QUAIL WITH SAUSAGE STUFFING

This is my favorite Christmas recipe. I've found that sausage-stuffed quail literally falls apart in the roux-infused gravy to create a thick and spicy bowl of wild deliciousness.

STUFFED QUAIL

4 whole quail, cleaned and partially deboned

1 tablespoon (15 ml) vegetable oil

2 pounds (910 g) fresh pork sausage

½ cup (80 g) finely diced yellow onion

½ cup (50 g) diced green onion tops

2 tablespoons (6 g) chopped flat-leaf parsley

2 tablespoons (16 g) minced garlic

2 tablespoons (6 g) chopped fresh rosemary

1 cup (200 g) cooked Louisiana long-grain white rice

STUFFED QUAIL

1. Preheat the oven to 350°F (180°C).

2. Rinse and dry the quail, being careful not to tear the flesh.

3. In a skillet over medium-high heat, add the oil. Add the sausage, yellow onion, and green onion and cook, breaking up the meat with a spatula, until browned, about 5 minutes. Add the parsley, garlic, rosemary, and cooked rice and stir to combine thoroughly. Stuff the mixture into the cavity of the quail, packing it full. Bring the two legs of the quail together and secure by tying with kitchen twine or with strips of aluminum foil. Repeat for each quail.

4. Place the quail on a baking sheet and cover with foil. Bake for 30 minutes and uncover. Bake for another 10 minutes or until the quail begin to brown on top. Remove the stuffed quail from the oven and remove the string. Keep warm until serving.

SIPPIN' SWEET TEA AND SPITTIN' SHOT

I cannot quell my passion for quail. I crave it when the first autumn leaves touch the ground, and no holiday would be complete without this quail recipe. Let me explain the source of my lifelong obsession for this tasty flight of fancy.

It all began when I was a kid growing up in small-town Louisiana. My Uncle Jerry—the closest thing I had to a grandfather—was an extraordinary fisherman and hunter who never hesitated to take me along for an adventure. We fished trotlines along the Pearl River and loaded the boat with catfish on many occasions. But it was his quail-hunting skills that captured the family's attention each and every holiday season.

My uncle hosted a Christmas Eve dinner every year. My aunt Lucy would fry up the quail and then smother them down into a stew infused with aromatic seasonings, pork sausage, and wild mushrooms.

I recall the ensuing family feeding frenzy interrupted only by the occasional discovery of birdshot against tooth. "That's how you know'd they're fresh kilt quail," my Uncle Jerry would proudly shout as another unfortunate family member bit into a 12-gauge BB. "No store-bought quail here, this is fresh-kilt," he'd chuckle as he announced to everyone who didn't hear him the first time.

The Christmas Eve quail dinner was a family tradition that brought together the Grahams to spin the stories of a generation. My dear uncle lived to see almost 90 holiday seasons, but like most family traditions, our quail dinners finally ended.

Now our Christmas Eve dinner tradition is quail after church services, and I can say that the memories made with family and friends are just as warm as I remember growing up. Quail is back on the Graham's holiday table and should be on yours as well.

GRAVY

1 tablespoon (15 ml) vegetable oil

1 cup (160 g) diced yellow onion

1 cup (150 g) diced green bell pepper

1 cup (120 g) diced celery

2 tablespoons (16 g) minced garlic

½ cup (25 g) chopped flat-leaf parsley

4 cups (960 ml) chicken stock

½ cup (120 ml) Dark Cajun Roux (page 230)

Kosher salt and freshly ground black pepper

1 cup (100 g) diced green onion tops

GRAVY

1. In a large cast-iron pot over medium-high heat, add the oil. When the oil is hot, add the onion, bell pepper, and celery. Sauté until the onion turns translucent, about 5 minutes. Add the garlic and parsley, and sauté until combined.

2. Add the chicken stock and bring to a boil, then add the roux. Decrease the heat to a simmer and cook for 30 minutes or until the roux has thickened the stock.

3. Sample the gravy and add salt and pepper to taste. Turn off the heat.

4. To serve, place a stuffed quail in the center of a large bowl and ladle the gravy around it. Garnish with the diced green onion.

WHOLE BRAISED OXTAIL WITH PEPPER JELLY GLAZE

Painted with a sweet and spicy glaze, and braised in a dark cauldron of flavor, this recipe will fire up your taste buds with fork-tender beefiness. But make no bones about it: oxtail is simply the tail end of a cow. The tail is made up of connective tissue and has lots of flavor, but it takes a long four-hour braise to break down the connective tissue and render this cut to fall-off-the-bone tenderness. Serve over rice or mashed potatoes.

1 (2½-pound [1.1 kg]) whole oxtail, cleaned

1 tablespoon (8 g) Cajun Seasoning Blend (page 231)

¼ cup (60 g) pepper jelly, divided

Coarsely ground black pepper

2 large spring onions with green stems attached

½ cup (80 g) sliced red onion

1 cup (50 g) chopped flat-leaf parsley, plus more for garnish

2 large carrots, cut into 1-inch (2.5 cm) chunks

2 bay leaves

6 mini sweet bell peppers, chopped and divided

1 tablespoon (8 g) minced garlic

1 cup (240 ml) dry red wine

2 cups (480 ml) beef stock

¼ cup (60 ml) Worcestershire sauce

½ cup (120 ml) dark soy sauce

1 tablespoon (18 g) sugarcane molasses, such as Steen's (see Sources, page 232)

2 tablespoons (16 g) cornstarch mixed with 2 tablespoons (30 ml) cold water

1 tablespoon (15 g) unsalted butter

Kosher salt

1. Preheat the oven to 300°F (150°C).

2. Cut the whole oxtail in half. Sprinkle all sides with the Cajun seasoning and brush with 2 tablespoons (30 g) of the pepper jelly. Sprinkle with black pepper.

3. In a Dutch oven with a heavy lid, add the oxtail. Add the onions, parsley, carrots, bay leaves, 4 of the sweet peppers, and garlic. Pour over the wine, stock, Worcestershire, soy sauce, and molasses to cover the oxtail halfway; if needed, add water to make up the difference. Cover and place in the oven. Cook until the meat is tender and pulls away from the bones, about 4 hours, basting and turning the meat every hour. Along the way, make sure there is plenty of liquid remaining; if not, add more water.

4. Remove the pot from the oven and uncover. Check for fork-tender meat, and if not, cook longer as needed. Transfer the oxtail to a serving platter along with the carrots from the pot. Keep warm.

5. Remove the vegetables from the braising liquid and skim any fat from the surface of the liquid. Return to the stovetop over medium-high heat and bring to a boil. Make a slurry with the cornstarch and cold water and add a couple of tablespoons (30 ml) to the braising liquid. As it boils, it will thicken and once it is of sauce consistency (to coat the back of a spoon), turn off the heat. Add the butter and stir into the sauce. Season to taste with salt and pepper. Remove the bay leaves.

6. Brush the oxtail with the remaining 2 tablespoons (30 g) pepper jelly and spoon over some of the sauce. Garnish with parsley and the remaining 2 peppers. Serve the remaining sauce on the side.

SERVES 4

PREP TIME: 40 MINUTES + DOUGHNUT DRYING AND SOAKING TIME
COOK TIME: 50 MINUTES
TOTAL TIME: 1 HOUR 30 MINUTES

DOUGHNUT BREAD PUDDING

Every town has its favorite doughnut shop that locals are obsessive about. So what could be better? How about a steaming dish of custardy bread pudding made from those little beauties drenched with a shot of warm bourbon cream sauce? Oh yeah, we're talking diet-destroying, highly addictive, nap-inducing, sugar buzz dessert here. If the thought of turning light-and-airy doughnuts into a pudding dessert leaves you glazed and confused, rest assured that it is well worth the effort.

BOURBON CREAM

1½ cups (360 ml) heavy cream

2 egg yolks

1 tablespoon (8 g) ground cinnamon

2 tablespoons (30 ml) bourbon

1 teaspoon vanilla extract

1 tablespoon (12 g) sugar

DOUGHNUT BREAD PUDDING

6 glazed doughnuts

6 eggs

2 cups (480 ml) half-and-half

3 tablespoons (24 g) ground cinnamon

1 tablespoon (8 g) ground nutmeg

1 tablespoon (15 ml) vanilla extract

½ teaspoon salt

3 tablespoons (54 g) dark sugarcane molasses

4 sprigs mint

BOURBON CREAM

1. In a heavy saucepan over medium-high heat, add the heavy cream and bring to a simmer. Lower the heat to maintain a simmer.

2. In a metal mixing bowl, add the egg yolks, cinnamon, bourbon, vanilla, and sugar. Whisk until thoroughly combined.

3. Slowly add a bit of the hot cream to the egg yolk mixture while whisking. Once the yolks have been tempered by the hot cream, add the entire mixture to the saucepan with the remaining cream. Gently simmer the mixture until it thickens enough to coat the back of a spoon, about 5 minutes. Keep warm for serving.

DOUGHNUT BREAD PUDDING

1. Break the doughnuts into bite-size pieces and place on the counter for at least 6 hours or overnight to dry out.

2. In a large mixing bowl, whisk the eggs with the half-and-half. Add the cinnamon, nutmeg, vanilla, salt, and molasses, and whisk to combine. Add the dried doughnut pieces to the mixture and submerge. Squeeze the doughnut pieces like a sponge to soak up the liquid. Place in the refrigerator overnight for best results.

3. Preheat the oven to 350°F (180°C). Coat four individual mini springform pans with nonstick spray. Line a baking sheet with foil. Divide pudding the mixture among the prepared pans and shake to release any air bubbles. Place the pans on the prepared baking sheet and place on the center rack of the hot oven. Bake until the tops are browned and a toothpick comes out clean, 30 to 40 minutes.

4. Pop out the bottom of the springform pans and transfer the puddings to individual dessert plates. Pool a bit of sauce on the bottom of the plate and serve the rest of the bourbon cream sauce on the side. Garnish each with a mint sprig.

SWEET POTATO PIE BRÛLÉE

If biting into a smooth and creamy slice of sweet potato pie with notes of cinnamon, cloves, nutmeg, and bourbon wasn't Thanksgiving enough, then pull out the blowtorch and blast away for a burnt sugar brûlée topping. This is one sweetie pie—Sweet Potato Pie Brûlée, to be exact.

PIE

3 large Louisiana sweet potatoes, baked until soft

¾ cup (180 ml) whole milk

¼ cup (60 ml) melted unsalted butter

4 large eggs, beaten

1 tablespoon (14 g) dark brown sugar

1 teaspoon honey, plus more for drizzling

1 teaspoon vanilla extract

¼ cup (60 ml) bourbon (optional)

¼ teaspoon ground cinnamon

¼ teaspoon ground cloves

¼ teaspoon freshly grated nutmeg

Pinch of salt

1 (9-inch [23 cm]) piecrust, homemade (page 66) or store-bought

8 thinly sliced sweet potato rounds

¼ cup water

PIE

1. Preheat the oven to 350°F (180°C).

2. Scoop out the flesh of the potatoes and mash with a fork until it is the consistency of a smooth purée. Remove any hard or stringy parts. Measure out 2 cups (480 g) of the mashed sweet potatoes and place in a large mixing bowl.

3. To the bowl, add the milk, butter, eggs, dark brown sugar, honey, vanilla, and bourbon (if using). Stir until smooth and lump-free. Season the mixture with the cinnamon, cloves, nutmeg, and salt.

4. Pour in enough of the mixture to fill the piecrust and place in the hot oven. Bake until the pie is set to a moist custardy consistency and the crust is browned, 45 to 60 minutes. (Watch the exposed top edge of the piecrust carefully and cover with a collar of aluminum foil if it begins to burn.) Remove the pie and refrigerate.

5. Meanwhile, place the rounds of sweet potato into a microwavable container. Add the water and cover the container loosely. Microwave on high and steam the sweet potato rounds until they soften and become fully cooked but still maintain their round shape, 3 to 5 minutes. Remove the slices from the container and drain on paper towels until dry.

LOUISIANA IS SWEET POTATO COUNTRY

The Louisiana Sweet Potato Commission is a division of the Louisiana Department of Agriculture and works to promote our crop, which is currently 20 percent of annual U.S. production. In 1987, Dr. Larry Ralston, an entomologist with LSU Agriculture Center's research branch, developed a more insect-resistant sweet potato and named it Beauregard. The Beauregard variety has a sweet, rich flavor, bakes well, and is why our sweet potatoes are known worldwide for quality.

BOURBON CREAM

2 cups (480 ml) whipping cream

1 tablespoon (12 g) granulated sugar

½ teaspoon ground cinnamon

2 tablespoons (30 ml) bourbon (optional)

1 tablespoon (14 g) light brown sugar

Mint leaves, for garnish

BOURBON CREAM

1. Place a stainless steel bowl in the freezer for 10 minutes. Add the whipping cream to the cold bowl. Add the granulated sugar, cinnamon, and bourbon (if using) and, using a hand mixer (or an immersion blender), whip the cream until stiff peaks form. Chill until ready to serve.

2. Blot dry the sweet potato rounds and place on top of the pie in a circular pattern, overlapping slightly; sprinkle evenly with the light brown sugar. Using a kitchen torch, hold the flame near the sugar and move it back and forth until the sugar begins to melt and caramelizes with burnt bits appearing, 1 minute or less. Stop short of blackening all of the sugar. Let the pie rest while the brûlée hardens. (If you do not own a culinary torch, carefully place the pie under the oven broiler while protecting the crust with an aluminum foil collar. Watch intently; it will only take seconds until browned.)

3. Remove the pie from the metal pie plate to a decorative cake stand. Slice into traditional wedges and place on individual dessert plates. Add a generous dollop of bourbon cream and drizzle the entire plate lightly with honey. Garnish with a mint leaf.

CHERRY BOUNCE

Deep, dark, and volatile is the most expressive way to describe this explosive elixir. It's Cherry Bounce—a tasty combination that plays on two of my favorite themes: Kentucky bourbon and ripe cherries. Just one sip of the smoky roundness of bourbon kissed with the sweet juice of dark cherries and it's time to celebrate.

This recipe is a textbook example of plan-ahead, delayed-gratification, kitchen experimentation at its best. It only takes a matter of minutes to make, but to enjoy it takes at least six months. Dark cherries, bourbon, and sugar complete the ingredient list, but time is what's most needed to work magic. Don't use the good stuff here: a blind taste test pitting Ancient Age bourbon against pricier upscale brands was an eye-opener that cheap can sometimes be better.

2 pounds (910 g) fresh sweet dark cherries, such as Bing

½ cup (100 g) sugar, such as caster

1 (750 ml) bottle bourbon

1. Clean and sterilize a 1-quart (960 ml) bottling jar following standard canning procedures.

2. Remove the stems from the cherries and wash thoroughly. Using a bamboo skewer, pierce both sides of the skin of the cherries so that the juices will run freely.

3. Pack the cherries in the jar, add the sugar, and cover completely with the bourbon.

4. Tightly screw on the lid and place in a cool part of the pantry for 6 months.

5. Open the jar and remove the cherries (freeze the marinated cherries to use later; ice cream sundae, anyone?). Pour the bounce over ice or enjoy straight up. Garnish with more fresh cherries and a sprig of mint, if you like.

6. For a spritzer variation, cut the Cherry Bounce with carbonated soda water or use your bounce to make the tastiest Old Fashioned ever. After opening, refrigerate your Cherry Bounce indefinitely.

RASPBERRY TRIFLE

The first bite stops you in your tracks. With just a smidgen of sweet liqueur soaking into the spongy cake, this delicate dessert bursts with the flavors of fresh berries against a tangy cream filling dusted with bittersweet chocolate. Oh yeah, this is a keeper!

1 large store-bought sponge cake, thickly sliced

6 tablespoons (90 ml) Grand Marnier liqueur, divided

¼ cup (60 ml) freshly squeezed orange juice

1 (14-ounce [397 g]) package madeleine cookies

2½ cups (600 ml) crema or whipped cream

2 tablespoons (25 g) sugar

2 cups (250 g) fresh raspberries

¼ cup (15 g) freshly grated bittersweet chocolate

Sprig of fresh mint

1. In a decorative glass trifle bowl, line the bottom with thick slices of sponge cake to come halfway up the side of the vessel. Drizzle the cake slices with ¼ cup (60 ml) of the liqueur and the orange juice.

2. Place the madeleine cookies along the edge of the glass bowl with the shell-shaped side facing outward.

3. In a small mixing bowl, stir together the crema, sugar, and remaining 2 tablespoons (30 ml) liqueur. Pour 2 cups (480 ml) of the crema into the center of the trifle bowl.

4. Arrange the raspberries on top of the crema and garnish with the remaining ½ cup (120 ml) crema. Sift over the grated chocolate and garnish with a sprig of mint. Chill for 1 hour and serve.

CAJUN BOUDIN

Make your own boudin from scratch or buy it online (see Sources, page 232).

1 (2-pound [910 g]) pork roast, fat trimmed

8 ounces (227 g) pork liver

1 cup (165 g) Louisiana long-grain white rice

1 large yellow onion, diced

2 tablespoons (16 g) minced garlic

2 tablespoons (16 g) Cajun Seasoning Blend (page 231)

1½ teaspoons cayenne pepper

1 bunch green onions, diced

Kosher salt and freshly ground black pepper

Dash of hot sauce

Casings (optional)

1. Preheat the oven to 400°F (200°C).

2. In a heavy pot with a tight-fitting lid, add the pork roast and fill the pot with water to a depth of 4 inches (10 cm). Cover, place in the hot oven, and braise the pork roast for 2 hours or until falling apart. Remove the pork from the pot, reserving the cooking liquid.

3. In a pot filled with water over high heat, add the liver and boil until well done, about 10 minutes. Remove and drain on a paper towel–lined plate.

4. In a rice cooker, make the rice following the package directions and keep warm until ready to use.

5. In a food processor, add the meat, liver, onion, and garlic and pulse until it reaches a smooth yet chunky consistency. Be careful not to overprocess to a pasty, mushy stage.

6. Incorporate the cooked rice in a ratio of 80 percent meat mixture to 20 percent rice. Gradually add some of the cooking liquid until the mixture is moist. Add the Cajun seasoning, cayenne, and green onions. Add salt, black pepper, and hot sauce to taste. Evenly incorporate the ingredients together.

7. Stuff the boudin into casings or wrap it tightly in aluminum foil. To keep warm, place it in a slow cooker set to warm with ½ inch (1.3 cm) of water in the bottom.

8. Another serving option is to shape the boudin into balls, dredge in cracker crumbs, and pan-fry for a Cajun delicacy.

DARK CAJUN ROUX

Make your own roux from scratch or order Rox's Roux online (see Sources, page 232).
Make sure you will have an hour of uninterrupted time, as you need to stir and watch the
pot constantly.

3 cups (360 g) all-purpose flour

3 cups (720 ml) vegetable, canola, or
peanut oil

1. In a large cast-iron pot over medium heat, add the flour and oil.

2. With a long-handled wooden spoon, begin to stir. Constant stirring of the flour around the bottom of the pot is key to browning the flour evenly to prevent burning. This early stage will go slowly as you begin to see the white flour take on a beige and then a tan color.

3. Continue stirring slowly and evenly, scraping the bottom and the circular crevices of the pot to move the flour around in the hot oil.

4. At about the 30-minute mark, you will begin to see a brown color developing and smell the first hints of toasted flour. This is where the stirring becomes even more crucial.

5. At this point, you begin to enter the phase where the least bit of inattention could result in burnt flecks of flour appearing—a sure sign you've ruined the roux. Watch your heat and lower it if the roux is cooking too fast.

6. Constant stirring to keep the flour from staying in one place too long prevents burning. You will begin to smell an even nuttier aroma as you see the color turn darker mahogany. Most stop here, but you will keep going until you achieve a deeper, darker chocolaty consistency and color.

7. Forget time at this point because you are now cooking by instinct, sight, and smell. The utmost attention is needed for your stirring, and when you see that chocolate darkness, you will know you have arrived.

8. Turn off the heat, but continue stirring until it begins to cool down and stops cooking.

9. Spoon the roux into a bowl and let cool. Refrigerate your roux in a glass jar for up to a year.

NOTES I like the neutral taste of vegetable or canola oil, and peanut oil will work fine as well, but stay away from olive oil, grapeseed oil, or any flavored oil with a low smoke point.

CAJUN SEASONING BLEND

This dry seasoning blend delivers a mix of distinct yet perfectly balanced spice components—all working in combination to deliver a wallop of Cajun flavor. And it's multipurpose: it infuses a deep, savory spiciness when added to the pot, it penetrates with a peppery punch when used as a rub, and it adds a zing when sprinkled on a finished dish.

¼ cup (72 g) salt

¼ cup (16 g) granulated garlic

¼ cup (32 g) finely ground black pepper

2 tablespoons (16 g) sweet paprika

2 tablespoons (12 g) onion powder

2 tablespoons (16 g) finely ground white pepper

1 tablespoon (18 g) celery salt

1 tablespoon (8 g) cayenne pepper

1. Add all of the ingredients to a food processor and blend. Pour into an airtight container and store at room temperature for up to 6 months.

NOTES The heat level is moderate, so feel free to add more cayenne, red pepper flakes, or hot sauce to your finished dish. This home-prepared blend does not contain the anti-caking compounds found in many commercial spice blends, so store it in a dry place.

SWEET HEAT SEASONING

My sweet heat seasoning blend combines a light brown sugar and cumin base with more familiar South Louisiana spices such as cayenne. It is a perfectly balanced spice rub that works well in a number of dishes from grilled pork chops to roasted butternut squash, and it should be a staple of your flavor arsenal.

2 tablespoons (28 g) light brown sugar

2 tablespoons (16 g) ground cumin

1 tablespoon (8 g) ground coriander

1 tablespoon (8 g) chili powder

1 tablespoon (8 g) sweet paprika

1 teaspoon ground cinnamon

1 teaspoon ground allspice

1 teaspoon ground ginger

½ teaspoon cayenne

½ teaspoon turmeric

½ teaspoon ground cloves

1. In a large mixing bowl, combine all the ingredients together and store in an airtight jar for up to 6 months.

SOURCES

When it comes to Louisiana cooking, authenticity is essential. Source fresh ingredients and high-quality products online from these fine Louisiana purveyors.

AL SIMON'S CAJUN MICROWAVES
(cajunmicrowaves.com)
Supplier of custom-made pig cookers

BAYOU RUM DISTILLERY
(bayourum.com)
Distillery specializing in a line of rums made from Louisiana sugarcane

BAYOU TECHE BREWING
(bayoutechebrewing.com)
Craft brewery making Ragin' Cajuns ale and other craft beers

THE BEST STOP
(beststopinscott.com)
Andouille, tasso, boudin, cracklins, and other sausage products

BILLEAUD'S MEAT AND GROCERY (billeauds.com)
Maker of smoked meats, tasso, stuffed chickens, boudin, and other Cajun products

BLUE PLATE (blueplatemayo.com)
Maker of mayonnaise products

BOSCOLI FOODS (boscoli.com)
Italian olive salad mix

CAJUNGROCER.COM
One-stop shopping for most Louisiana products, such as pickled quail eggs, pickled pork, andouille, tasso, pepper jellies, hot sauces, dry seasonings, meats, crawfish tail meat, frog legs, alligator, and seafood

CAJUN POWER
(cajunpowersauce.com)
Line of sauces and prepared foods

CAMELLIA BRAND
(camelliabrand.com)
Line of dried beans and peas

CANE RIVER PECAN COMPANY
(caneriverpecan.com)
Line of pecan products and gift items

CERTIFIED LOUISIANA
(certifiedlouisiana.org) Listings of authentic Louisiana and Cajun food products from the Louisiana Department of Agriculture

D'ARTAGNAN MEATS
(dartagnan.com)
Guinea hen, duck, rabbit, and lamb

DON'S SPECIALTY MEATS
(donsspecialtymeats.com)
Andouille, tasso, boudin, cracklins, and other sausage products

FELICIANA CELLARS WINERY
(felicianacellars.com)
Muscadine wine

HEBERT'S SPECIALTY MEATS
(hebertsmaurice.com)
Deboned stuffed chickens, turducken, andouille, tasso, boudin, quail, rabbit, and other meats

JACOB'S WORLD FAMOUS ANDOUILLE (cajunsausage.com)
Maker of andouille, hog's head cheese, and smoked meats

LOUISIANA DIRECT SEAFOOD
(louisianadirectseafood.com)
Shrimp, crabmeat, oysters, crawfish tail meat, black drum, wild-caught catfish, red snapper, flounder, and other seafood

ROX'S ROUX (acadianatable.com)
Dark Cajun roux in a jar

SAZERAC COMPANY (sazerac.com)
Distillery featuring absinthe, praline liqueur, and other Louisiana specialties

STEEN'S SYRUP MILL
(steenssyrup.com)
Sugarcane syrup and molasses

SUPREME RICE
(supremerice.com)
Line of rice products

SWAMP POP SODA
(drinkswamppop.com)
Line of six different flavored sodas, including Praline Cream Soda

TABASCO (tabasco.com)
Maker of pepper sauces, pepper jelly, and other Louisiana products

T-BOY'S MEATS (tboysboudin.com)
Boudin, sausage, tasso, and other Cajun meats

ZAPP'S (zapps.com)
Maker of a line of spicy potato chips

ZATARAIN'S (zatarains.com)
Creole mustard, crab boil, and spices

ACKNOWLEDGMENTS

As a writer, I am truly blessed to have the encouragement of my wife, Roxanne. For every story you've told, every roux you've stirred, and every dish you've washed, I am forever grateful.

A heartfelt thank you to my daughter, Lauren, who continues to inspire my creativity with her wide-eyed enthusiasm that drives me to discover new talents.

Much appreciation to the in-law side of my extended family: To Rosalie Waldrop, Rhonda Waldrop, and Reverend Jesse Waldrop, who are an endless source of colorful stories and delicious Cajun cooking.

To the Grahams, wherever you are and whatever you're cooking: Our proud heritage of life around the kitchen table lives on for the next generation.

Thank you to all of my Graham Group team of professionals: Michelle Constantin for being the rock that anchors me, Kathy Andersen for leadership, Raymond Credeur for creative brilliance when I need it, and to art director Kerry Palmer for always having the answers. And to Julia Marks and Beth Perry for keeping it all flowing smoothly.

To The Harvard Common Press/Quarto Publishing Group pros who have worked tirelessly to make this book the best possible. Thanks especially go to editorial project manager Jessi Schatz for managing the workflow and keeping me on track, creative director Regina Grenier for a dazzling design, and senior marketing manager Todd Conly for making sure the world knows about this book.

A very special thank you goes to editorial director Dan Rosenberg for believing in this book and shepherding it through to completion.

And most notably, thanks to my literary agent Judy Linden, executive vice president at Stonesong, for believing in my talent. And much appreciation to her entire team for continuing to help me navigate the publishing world.

A thank you to Louisiana growers, processors, fishers, home cooks, and chefs who are passionate about their craft and help make our Cajun and Creole food culture so unique.

I appreciate all the readers of my food blog and first cookbook, *Acadiana Table* for the valuable feedback and endless insight into my recipes and stories that help me be a better writer.

And thanks to God for blessing me with the talent to tell the stories of my Louisiana.

ABOUT THE AUTHOR

When George Graham sinks his teeth into a juicy story, you can be assured it will be in good taste. He is a food writer that is curious about his subject and passionate about his craft. An award-winning writer, cook, and photographer, he is the author of *Acadiana Table: Cajun and Creole Home Cooking from the Heart of Louisiana*, a 320-page collection of stories and recipes published in 2016 by Harvard Common Press.

Louisiana is his home, and here he documents the region's culture and culinary traditions. He writes for newspapers and magazines, and he has been a finalist on television's *Food Network Challenge*. In 2013 he launched the blog *Acadiana Table*, which has been a finalist for Best Food Blog: Regional Cuisine in *Saveur* magazine's 2014 Best Food Blog Awards and also for Best Food Blog in 2015 and 2017 IACP Digital Media Awards. His food photography has appeared in the museum exhibit *Feast for the Eyes: A History of Food in Photography* at the Louisiana Arts and Science Museum.

He writes from Lafayette, Louisiana, where he lives with his wife and daughter.